MYSTERIES OF
THE MIND

AN EYE TO THE FUTURE

MYSTERIES OF THE MIND

BLITZ EDITIONS

Published by Blitz Editions
an imprint of Bookmart Ltd
Registered Number 2372865
Trading as Bookmart Ltd, Desford Road, Enderby
Leicester LE9 5AD

Cover design: Peter Dolton
Text design: Jim Reader
Production Manager: Sue Gray
Editorial Manager: Roz Williams

Printed in the Slovak Republic
50974

ISBN 1 85605 129 3

Every effort has been made to contact the copyright holders for the pictures.
In some cases they have been untraceable, for which we offer our apologies.
Thanks to the Fortean Picture Library and the Hulton Deutsch Collection Ltd, who supplied most of them.
Pictures have been provided as follows: M. De Cet (p 7), Hulton Deutsch Collection Ltd (pp 2–4, 5 middle,
6, 10, 11, 14, 15, 17–21, 22–3 bottom, 24, 28–33, 34 top, 35–8, 42, 43 top left and right, 45 top,
63 bottom, 67–70, 74), McDonnell Douglas Photos (p 5 top), The Mansell Collection (p 22),
Mary Evans Picture Library (pp 77, 80) and *Psychic News* (p 60).
The remainder have been supplied by the Fortean Picture Library.
Cover: The Hulton Deutsch Collection Ltd supplied the pictures at top and middle right
and the picture on the back. The remainder were supplied by the Fortean Picture Library.

The Author
Reuben Stone has long been fascinated by the paranormal
and the mysteries of the unexplained. He is the author of many books
and articles on military history, popular science and technology,
and various aspects of anomalous phenomena.

The young aristocrat's dreams had proved correct in the past. If he trusted his erratic gift this time he stood to win a fortune – or lose one.

After serving gallantly in World War 2, the young aristocrat, the Hon. John Raymond Godley, went up to Balliol College, Oxford. On the night of 8 March 1946, he dreamed that he was reading the next day's evening paper. Among the racing results he noted that a horse named Brindal and another named Juladin had both won their respective races at odds of 7–1.

The next day he met a friend and told him about the dream. The pair checked two daily papers, and found that Brindal was running in the 1 pm race at Plumpton that afternoon, while Juladin was running at Wetherby in the 4 pm race. Godley's dream, however, had been optimistic: Brindal's starting price was 5–4, and Juladin's 5–2. He put money on Brindal, which won, and then put his winnings on Juladin, which also won. Several of Godley's friends, hearing about his dream, had put money on one or other of the horses too.

Rather than being elated at the accuracy of his precognition and the pleasure of winning his bets, Godley was actually rather worried at the outcome. In the next few weeks, his mornings were disturbed by people asking him if he'd had any good tips in his dreams. This bothered him: he reasoned that if he did have such a dream again, and his friends put money on his premonition – and *then lost their money*, he would be mightily, and rightly, unpopular.

But no more dreams came for nearly a month, by which time Godley was safe at his father Lord Kilbracken's isolated home in Ireland for the Easter vacation. On the night of 4 April he again dreamed of reading a list of winners; the only name he recalled on waking was Tubermore. The family house was so remote that the papers arrived days late, so Godley used the telephone to discover that a horse called Tuberose was running in the Grand

When he was a student at Balliol College, Oxford (above), in 1946, John Godley had the first of a series of dreams that could have turned into a bookies' nightmare: he accurately foresaw the winners of two races, one at Plumpton (opposite) and the other at Wetherby. Such dreams continued intermittently over the years and included several winners of the Grand National (below).

Right: *Mr What wins the Grand National in 1958 – as John Godley's dream had foretold. But this was the last occasion on which Godley's unlikely gift was to make him any money.*

FRIENDS BESIEGED HIM FOR HIS RACING TIPS – BUT IF THE HORSES LOST GODLEY FEARED HE WOULD BE VILIFIED.

National that day. The name was near enough to the dream horse for Godley and his family to back it. The evening news on the radio told them Tuberose had won.

The next time Godley dreamed of a winning horse, the following July, the image that came to him was not of a newspaper, but of a telephone booth at the Randolph Hotel in Oxford, from which he was checking the result of a race with his bookie; the time after that – a year later, in July 1947 – he dreamed he saw the winner come in, and even recognized the jockey. In both cases his dreams came true, and he made money.

Godley's gift was erratic and irregular in its appearances, but it rarely let him down – until, in 1958, he had his last successful punter's dream winner (and bookie's nightmare). He won £450 (the equivalent today of about £7000) on an outsider in the Grand National. After that, he dreamed of no more winners.

John Godley's gift was at once typical of precognition in general, and highly unusual. It was typical in that the information he received about the future was often not strictly accurate. The names of the real-life horses were frequently slightly different from those he dreamed – his biggest win ever, and his last, came from a horse named Mr What, running in the Grand National, but the name he dreamed was 'What Man'. Typical too was the spasmodic fashion in which these dreams arrived, and the abrupt way they stopped. Godley could hardly have made a living out of his premonitions,

for they simply did not come often enough.

What is peculiar about them is their consistency when they did come, and their highly specialized nature (when they began, Godley was only mildly interested in racing) – and they are most unusual in *continuing* to occur. Most precognitions of such a specific kind come once or twice in a lifetime. Even 'professional' psychics, whose premonitions are usually much more general in nature, rarely have such runs of precise, repetitive and particular visions from the future.

A CLOSE SHAVE WITH DEATH

Precognition in general, however, is a recognized branch of extra-sensory perception, and like all parapsychological phenomena raises endless questions – both about the mysterious mechanics of how the human mind can read the future, and about the nature of time itself. Both these problems arise when people foresee disasters.

One of the best-attested and documented instances of a precognition of a disaster was first made known to one of its victims at a cocktail party. The night before he was due to fly home from Shanghai in January 1946, Air Marshal Sir Victor Goddard of the Royal New Zealand Air Force was invited to a gathering hosted by the British Consul-General, G.A. Ogden. In the midst of the general chatter, Goddard was suddenly distracted by someone behind him saying, 'Too bad about Goddard.

Left: *Air Marshal Sir Victor Goddard, whose crash in a DC-3 Dakota* (above) *was foreseen by a British naval officer, later Admiral Sir Gerald Gladstone.*

Terrible crash.'

Goddard turned round in amazement. The speaker – a Royal Navy officer named Gerald Gladstone – recognized Goddard and froze. 'I'm terribly sorry – I mean,' he stammered, 'I'm terribly glad.' Then Gladstone (he was later to be Admiral Sir Gerald Gladstone) explained that he had had an unbidden, overwhelmingly powerful vision of Goddard in a DC-3 ('Dakota'). In his vision, the plane ran into a snowstorm, flew over mountains and then crashed in failing light on a shingly shore. All aboard were killed. The passengers, apart from Goddard, included three civilians: two Englishmen and a girl.

Goddard was no stranger to psychic experiences and did not mock Gladstone's vision. But he felt he had no need to worry. He was indeed about to fly the first leg of his journey, to Tokyo, in a DC-3, but he was taking only two of his staff officers.

But by the end of the party he had gathered three further passengers. The Consul-General, G.A. Ogden, had an urgent message requesting him to be in Tokyo as soon as possible for a meeting; Goddard offered him a seat on his plane. A London *Daily Telegraph* reporter, Seymour Berry, then begged a lift. Finally, Tokyo sent a further request – for a secretary to take minutes of the meeting. Miss Dorita Breakspear became the third civilian on the flight.

Goddard's DC-3 – named *Sister Ann*, it was Supreme Allied Commander, South-East Asia, Lord Louis Mountbatten's personal aircraft – took off for Tokyo next morning. At about 3 pm, it began to run into snow, and the radio failed. When the *Sister Ann* finally crossed the coast of Japan, the crew was confronted unexpectedly by mountains. The plane was low on fuel, and clearly well off course. The pilot decided to look for somewhere to land the plane as safely as possible.

True to Gladstone's premonition, there was a snowstorm raging as the plane came out under the cloud cover. Ditching in the sea, whipped up by the storm, was out of the question. But below them they saw a small village, and a strip of shingly shore. Goddard was now sure that every detail of Gladstone's vision would come true.

The pilot made three attempts to land on the narrow beach. The last succeeded, but the plane spun across the shingle, its undercarriage collapsing. When it came to rest facing the sea, Goddard was amazed to

GODDARD REALIZED THAT EVERY DETAIL OF THE PREMONITION HAD COME TRUE, AND AS THE PLANE CRASHED ONTO THE SHINGLE, HE KNEW THAT HIS DEATH WAS INEVITABLE.

find himself still alive – as were all the other passengers and crew. They had landed on Sado Island, some 200 miles north of Tokyo, and on the other side of the Japanese mainland from the capital.

Gladstone's distressing vision had been right in all respects but one: those on board had lived to confirm the details of his premonition. Crucial though the difference was to those who survived, some

Someone, somewhere, will always have an accurate premonition of major events. The sinking of the liner **Titanic** *in April 1912* (**above**) *and the Allied campaign in France after D-Day* (**below**) *were foreseen by a host of people.*

parapsychologists would argue that this does not invalidate Gladstone's experience as a genuine precognition.

The theory behind this assertion is easier to understand when you realize that a certain kind of premonition of disaster is *always* incomplete.

A number of people, for example, cancelled their passage on the ill-fated *Titanic* after premonitions that the ship would sink. One, a Mr Conan Middleton, had two dreams in which he saw the liner floating capsized. Another, Colin Macdonald, would have taken a step up in his career had he taken the job of second engineer that he was offered on the doomed ship. None of these glimpses of the future actually *prevented* the disaster that overtook the *Titanic* on the night of 12 April 1912, although the chances are that precognition did alter the future for those who had them, and acted on their hunches and refused to sail: roughly seven in every ten people on board died after the ship hit an iceberg in the North Atlantic.

PHANTOM ORDERS

To take a more recent instance of a premonition of disaster that saved the life

of the percipient, Mr Chris Ross of Hove, Sussex, described in the early 1980s what happened when his father was driving a truck loaded with ammunition in a convoy across France some time after D-Day in 1944. For the duration of the journey, the men had been ordered to sleep in their trucks during rest stops. In the first such stop, Ross's father had been asleep for an hour or so when he was woken up by someone shouting an order: 'Get that truck out of here, quickly!'

The soldier did as he was told, automatically – then stopped after a few hundred yards, mystified at the fact that he alone had started up and pulled out. The next thing he saw was a pair of Messerschmitt fighters flying straight at the parked convoy through a gap in the nearby hills. After they had done their brief but nasty work, three trucks were out of action and several men lay dead.

Ross then found himself being quizzed by the unit's commander about why he had driven off – it was impossible for him to have seen the two enemy planes coming. Ross replied that he had simply obeyed the order he'd heard – only to be told that no such order had been given. When the two men returned to the convoy, they found a bomb crater precisely where Ross's ammunition truck had been parked. The phantom order – or premonition – had prevented the bomb hitting the ammunition truck and, no doubt, killing many more men than the convoy actually lost.

Nonetheless, there was nothing Ross could have done to stop the Messerschmitts attacking; his premonition (which, one presumes, was cannily interpreted by his subconscious to take the form most likely to get an unquestioning response) and his prompt action certainly saved lives. But Ross did not, in a sense, foresee the future: he saw what *would* inevitably happen if he did not act in a certain way, and quickly.

Something like Ross's dramatized flash of intuition must have occurred to the anonymous young man described by Mr E.J. Branwell in a letter written in the early 1980s. One day in the late 1970s, Branwell was in Peter Robinson's department store in Oxford Street, London, when he saw a young man appear as if from nowhere, running furiously toward an 'up' escalator between two floors of the store. On the

escalator were two women and a child in a pushchair, riding to the next floor. The young man leapt up the escalator, and as he got to 'within three steps' of the group, the pushchair slipped and the child fell out – into his arms. The witness noted that other people who saw this happen were amazed at the speed of the young man's reaction; but, he asked pointedly: 'How can you have a reaction to something that hasn't happened?'

Some forms of precognition, then, are not precise pictures of the future, as if the course of coming events is inevitable and immutable, like John Godley's (sometimes hazy) precognitions of winners of horse

Above: A Messerschmitt ME-109 of the type that fired on a convoy of British Army trucks in 1944 – and whose attack was foreseen by one of the convoy's drivers.

ROSS OBEYED THE ORDER INSTINCTIVELY – ONLY TO FIND HE'D LEFT HIS CONVOY BEHIND AND THE MESSERSCHMITTS WERE MOVING IN FOR THE KILL.

races. These premonitions are intimations of potential events, whether involving their percipients or others. But the *general* pattern of events is unchanged. The *Titanic* still sailed from Southampton, and sank; the Messerschmitts still flew, and a number of British soldiers died as a result, unaware of their approach; the child still fell from its pushchair at Peter Robinson's store.

Gladstone's 'vision' of Goddard's death was *itself* no different from these examples: he foresaw the *potential* results of a crashed aircraft and some very accurate details of the circumstances of the crash. He begged Goddard not to fly to Japan the next day; Goddard felt safe in doing so – even though, as it turned out, detail by detail of Gladstone's precognition emerged as accurate. Precisely why he may have been wrong about the final, critical detail – the death of the passengers and crew on board that plane – we shall consider later.

POINTLESS WARNING

Crises in the future are clearly significant in generating premonitions – and perhaps for obvious reasons. We mark our lives by crises – the highs and lows of getting on with living. Few people are not touched emotionally to some degree by major disasters, however distant their connections with those dead, maimed or fortunate enough to escape.

But by that token, everyone 'ought' to have premonitions of major events affecting their own and others' lives; and yet most of us go through life with not an inkling of the personal disasters that will befall us as individuals, let alone the horrors that may confront hundreds or even thousands of our fellow humans caught up in a plane crash, an earthquake, or some similar calamity. The arbitrary, infuriating and mysterious nature of premonitions (and of ESP in general) is nowhere more obvious than in the very obscurity and uselessness of some of them.

Mrs Marjory Walker of Harrietsham, Kent, was struck in 1950 by an extraordinarily vivid dream that she had while on holiday that year. 'I dreamed,' she recounted, 'I was looking at a scene in a busy London street, complete with tramlines [then a feature of the London scene], vehicles and a crowd of people who were gathered around a body on the ground. Next I found myself looking at the right-hand column of the front page of the *Daily Express*. It read: "Stuart Andrew Walker, aged 8 1/2 years [the name and age of one of my sons], falls to death from the balcony of his parents' London flat."'

Some time later, the *Daily Express* featured a report of a child's death in precisely the place Mrs Walker had foreseen it, and with a picture of exactly the scene she had dreamed. But the report read: 'Hilary Page's 2 1/2-year-old daughter, one of twin girls, falls to her death from the balcony of her parents' flat.'

'Why,' asked Mrs Walker reasonably enough, yet with obvious pain, 'should I have a dream so similar to an actual tragedy, yet about the wrong child so that I could not warn the family in time...why did I have that dream at all when it proved of no use to anyone?'

What makes this story additionally curious is that Mrs Walker's second son (not the one who featured in her dream) in due course became a successful businessman and bought the company owned by Hilary Page (who had invented the Kiddicraft range of educational toys). So there was a connection between the two families lying in the future: although Mrs Walker's premonition was garbled and useless, it does suggest that there was some kind of attraction across time between them that expressed itself in this particularly frustrating way.

MAGIC RITUALS

Still more frustrating – and perplexing – are those few instances of premonitions that amount to major prophecies – and that no one at the time registers as such. The most often quoted instance of seemingly accurate prophecy of this kind is the vast body of obscure quatrains published by the French physician and clairvoyant Michel Nostradamus (1503–1566).

Nostradamus reputedly gathered the material for these verses by 'scrying' nightly in his study. He began each session with a magic ritual, setting a bowl of water in a brass tripod on his desk, touching the tripod with a wand and dipping the wand into the water, after which he touched the tip of the wand to his robe. He would then settle down to record what he saw and heard – visions that came to him, he said, 'by the subtle spirit of fire', in a fragmented form and accompanied by a disembodied voice that, he believed, was the Divine Presence in limbo (the region of the afterlife that, in Roman Catholic doctrine, houses the souls of the unbaptized).

The peculiar obscurity of the results of this ritual has been ascribed to Nostradamus's fear of the Inquisition, which had paid him some unwanted attention in the past; to avoid any suspicion of dabbling in witchcraft he wrote in a patchwork of Greek, Latin, French, and local Provençal dialect, and liberally sprinkled his visionary text with what later interpreters construed as anagrams. Other obscurities – a famous one is the similarity between the name 'Hister' and the name 'Hitler' – have been put down to the corruption of details so common in premonitions.

Nostradamus has been credited with a truly astonishing range of accurate predictions. According to Marion Zimmer Bradley's *Encyclopedia of Mystical & Paranormal Experience* these include foreseeing the Napoleonic wars; the history of the British monarchy from Elizabeth I to Elizabeth II – including the abdication of Edward VIII; the American revolutionary and civil wars; the rise and fall of Hitler; the assassinations of US Presidents Lincoln and Kennedy; and even the rise of the Ayatollah Khomeini in Iran. He predicted air and space travel, the use of submarines in warfare, and the development of the atomic bomb.

Some of Nostradamus's quatrains indeed appear to be startlingly precise and accurate about events that were to occur long after the publication of his verses. He did, for instance, predict the date of the French Revolution, and described a particular event that would follow: 'By night will come into Varennes through the forest of Reines two married people, by a circuitous route, Herne the white stone, the black Monk in grey, the elected Capet; and the result will be tempest, fire, blood, slice [*tempeste, feu, sang, tranche*].'

On 20 June 1792, Louis Capet – King Louis XVI, who was in fact elected to the throne he had inherited by the revolutionary Constituent Assembly – and his wife Marie Antoinette disguised themselves (he in grey, she in white) and fled from Paris in an attempt to reach their army of supporters near Rheims (Reines). The royal pair took a circuitous route to Rheims by way of Varennes – which was where they were arrested. The attempt at flight discredited Louis entirely, and led directly to the Reign of Terror in which the 'slice' of the guillotine played so prominent a part. That tireless instrument of death indeed ended Louis's and Marie Antoinette's own lives in the summer and autumn respectively of the following year.

Below: *Nostradamus, whose predictions in obscure verse have been the object of fascinated study for over 400 years.*

Above: *Inflation of the German currency reached almost surreal heights in the 1920s – an event prophesied by an obscure French civilian captured on the Western Front in August 1914, when the German empire was at its most powerful.*

All this is very impressive; but the accuracy and truth of Nostradamus's words are apparent only *after* the events they describe have occurred. And some details still trouble even the sympathetic modern reader: who, or what, is Herne the (white) stone? By what stretch of the imagination could King Louis XVI be called a black monk? Apart from these nagging points, there is little in the quatrain itself that unambiguously says that the King of France and his wife would be caught trying to escape from Paris in 1792, and predicts the invention and the industrious application of the guillotine.

This is not to say that Nostradamus did not foresee these very events: but he did

not say so very clearly. The difficulty we are left with is how to determine, from his somewhat less than limpid language, exactly what Nostradamus may have been predicting would happen during any particular period that still remains in the future; and when the details seem clear, the dating of them is frequently not.

The quatrains are so obliquely written that no one has actually been able to use them as predictions until events have already occurred to bear them out. Before 1990 it would have been hard to point with any certainty to what he may have foreseen concerning, for example, the former Soviet Union in the early 1990s. This will not stop those who wish to from finding a suitable set of lines that seems to predict the fall of the Soviet empire – but it will be hindsight, not Nostradamus's precognition, that reveals them.

TERRIFYING ACCURACY

Far more specific, and far more astonishing in their clarity and precision, are the prophetic words of another Frenchman, reported in the 'Rill letters' from World War 1.

Andreas Rill was by training a carpenter; he came from Untermuhlhausen in Bavaria. In August 1914 he was on active service with the German army, and his unit was billeted in a Capuchin monastery near Colmar, Alsace. From here he wrote two letters to his family about the extraordinary predictions that a French prisoner had made while being questioned by Rill and his fellow-soldiers.

Rill described the prisoner – who does not seem to have been a soldier, but a French citizen who simply got in the way of the Kaiser's army – as 'a strange holy man who said incredible things'. Much

The anonymous Frenchman foretold the rise of Hitler (above, with Mussolini) and his defeat (left – British, US and Soviet troops celebrate the fall of Berlin in 1945), along with a host of other startlingly accurate details of the Nazi regime.

later, in the 1980s, Rill's son Siegmund told investigators that his father had maintained that the Frenchman had told him that he had once been a rich man and a Freemason, but had given away his wealth and joined the monastery. Among this visionary's predictions were the following:

• The war they were fighting would last five years.

• Germany would lose the war.

• A revolution would follow the war in Germany.

• Everyone in Germany would become a millionaire; indeed 'there would be so much money that it would be thrown out of windows and no one would bother to pick it up' [Andreas Rill commented that this was 'ridiculous!'].

• During this time the Antichrist would be born, and around 1932 would become a tyrannical dictator over Germany for approximately nine years.

• In 1938, preparations for war would begin.

• The war would last three years and end with the downfall of the dictator – 'the man and his sign will disappear'.

• After the war, things 'that are simply inhuman' would be discovered about the dictator's regime.

• In 1945 Germany would be 'pressed from all sides and totally plundered and destroyed'.

• Foreign powers would occupy Germany, but the country would recover economically.

• Italy would fight against Germany in this war [i.e. World War 1] but with Germany in the next war.

The accuracy of these predictions is astonishing. World War 1 lasted only four years and three months, but in August 1914 the word on everyone's lips, on both sides, was that it would be over by Christmas. As everyone knows, the Germans lost, and there was a revolution in Germany. Phenomenal inflation in the early 1920s made everyone in Germany a 'millionaire'. 'Around 1932' is not a bad guess for the establishment of Hitler's power: the Nazi party swept to power in elections held in January 1933. World War 2 lasted longer than three years, although it was clear that Germany could not win it by the end of 1942.

The natural conclusion of a sceptic

would be that the letters were forged after World War 2. But Dr Hans Bender of the Freiburg Institute in Germany had them examined by forensic scientists for signs of fraud or later changes, and they found none; while Rill's son – who was born in 1906 – recounted how the predictions in his letters were well known around Unter-muhlhausen between the wars. Dr Bender's researchers also cross-checked other details of the letters with existing records and concluded they were authentic.

But who was the mysterious French prophet?

Dr Bender's investigators used the war journal of the unit in which Andreas Rill served to establish that in August 1914 part of Rill's company had billeted at a Capuchin monastery in Sigolsheim, six miles from Colmar. Another key fact was that in 1918, Rill's unit had returned to the Colmar area and had been stationed in Turckheim, some eight miles from Sigolsheim. Rill took the opportunity to walk the distance in the hope of seeing the visionary again, but on arriving there he was told that the Frenchman had died earlier in the year.

Checking the monastery's records – and those of all the Capuchin houses in the area – the researchers found no record of a French monk who had died in 1918, but they did discover that at Sigolsheim an official *guest* – known as a Frater Laicus Tertiarius – of the monastery there had died that year, and before Rill's visit. A rich man (who may well have given his wealth to the order) and one who was also a Freemason would not have had difficulty in being accepted as a permanent guest with the order, the investigators believed. Although they were unable to establish that this was precisely the man they were looking for, they felt satisfied that the Rill letters were indeed authentic.

In this extraordinary case we are confronted yet again with predictions that are startlingly accurate, mingled with others whose details are imprecise or at least less accurate than others. And some of the French prophet's precognitions – which we have not dwelt on here, and they were markedly fewer than his accurate predictions – were simply wrong. But so too have details in the other cases we have looked at here been wrong. Is there any explanation for this? Or any explanation for cases like that of Mrs Walker, whose premonition was, as we said, garbled and useless, although it was accurate in many points of detail and did indeed concern someone who, in the future, would play a major part in the life of one of her sons?

SIGNALS FROM THE FUTURE

To account for precognition of any kind we are forced to speculate about the nature of time. The only possible explanation for accurate precognition is that it is possible, by some inexplicable means, to see into the future. But the real question is: which future?

There is no reason, the experts tell us, to believe that there is only one possible future. Both physicists and theologians would agree on that point. The physicists go one stage further, and suggest that time may constantly be splitting up into different 'timelines' and, indeed, even into separate universes *all the time*. To some extent we may each of us be living in a private universe, but one that is intimately related – indeed barely distinguishable – to the universes of most other people.

A precognition of a future event may be 99 per cent accurate and yet its key feature not come true – as in the case of Admiral Gladstone's vision of Air Marshal Goddard's death. Some scientists would argue that Goddard did die – but not in this timeline or in this universe. What Gladstone saw was an event from a parallel universe, obviously one that shared most of the features of the one in which this story is told. In that parallel reality, Gladstone's precognition may be celebrated as an all too accurate picture of what was to come. In yet another reality, the precognition will have been forgotten, because Goddard took his flight alone, as he had assumed he would, and landed safely in Tokyo.

But if these different realities do exist, it would be surprising if the more similar ones did not suffer from a certain amount of 'cross-talk' – like the dim echo of a different conversation, running parallel to our own, that we hear occasionally on the telephone, or as the left-hand channel of a stereo picks up sound that is intended for the right-hand loudspeaker.

The signal from the future – from this timeline or any other – is not strong, however, and the information that individuals pick up can be strangely distorted. But the 'parallel universe' hypothesis might itself explain this lack of clarity – in radio or hi-fi terms, this high signal-to-noise ratio. Until we find a way of crossing these barriers, it is unlikely that many precognitions will be as useful as John Godley's were to him.

Above: *The late Dr Hans Bender. A team from his research institute in Freiburg, Germany, verified the authenticity of the prophetic 'Rill letters' and almost succeeded in identifying the author of their astonishingly accurate predictions.*

A MEETING OF MINDS

The professor's telepathic gifts told him that his daughter's life hung on a thread, but he was powerless to do anything to help her.

Ernst Cassirer, who died in 1945 at the age of 70, was one of the 20th century's most humane and creative philosophers. He was also psychic, in one specific way: he always knew, without being told, when his daughter Anna was ill. On three or four occasions, she told psychical researcher and scholar Lawrence LeShan, during the years she was at boarding school in Germany, Cassirer woke up in the middle of the night and insisted on telephoning her school. Each time, he was told that Anna had been taken ill and was in the school sanatorium. He never, she said, called in this way when she was well – which was most of the time.

In 1919 Cassirer became professor of philosophy at the University of Hamburg, and remained there until Hitler came to power in Germany in 1933. During this time Anna grew up and left home to study in Berlin. While she was a student, Cassirer came to visit her; they spent an evening at a party together, and the next day Cassirer caught the train back to Hamburg. The express made only one stop on the journey, at Wittenberg. As it pulled in, Cassirer grabbed his suitcase, jumped off the train, and at once telephoned his daughter's lodgings in Berlin.

'What happened?' he demanded of the housekeeper. 'What is the matter with Anna?'

He was told she had been taken to hospital. Cassirer called the infirmary at once, and learned that only an hour after he had caught his train home, she had begun to haemorrhage. She was now in emergency surgery.

Cassirer's experiences are good instances of telepathy at work. And they are typical, too, of telepathy in Western

societies – which for the majority of us seems to occur most often as a spontaneous response to a crisis. A few gifted individuals do seem able to 'tune in' to other minds at will, and some have tried to train and develop these powers. But they are few and far between – and far less common in the industrial West than they are in so-called 'primitive' tribal societies.

Why this should be the case may offer some clues as to *what* telepathy is, even if the mystery of how it works remains unsolved. And it may help explain why laboratory experiments into telepathy have not been consistent or entirely successful.

MIND READING

Frederic Myers, like his famous near-contemporary Matthew Arnold, was an erudite inspector of schools and a poet; born in 1843, he was also one of the founders of the Society for Psychical Research. It was he who coined the term 'telepathy', defining it as 'the communication of impressions of any kind from one mind to another independently of the recognized channels of the senses'.

Since the SPR was founded in 1882, there have been literally thousands of experiments in psychology laboratories around the world, all dedicated to establishing the reality of telepathy. The

The free and easy movement of a Masai dancer (opposite) contrasts with the formality of a Western city such as Hamburg (above), where Ernst Cassirer, philosopher and occasional telepathist, lived before World War 2. Does the human mind have a built-in capacity for telepathic communication – one that flourishes in so-called 'primitive' societies but only occasionally bursts forth in 'civilized' cultures?

experiments have become more and more sophisticated over the years, but the data that have been collected from them have failed to convince mainstream scientists that telepathy actually exists at all. The parapsychologists who have designed and conducted these experiments would disagree, but even the most dedicated and 'believing' of them would agree that none of this work has got anyone closer to understanding *how* telepathy works.

The reasons for this strange and unsatisfactory state of affairs are various. Not least among them is the stubborn conviction among many orthodox scientists that *all* paranormal phenomena are simply 'impossible' because they break the known laws of science. The logic, such as it is, of this argument runs approximately as follows: science has no way to explain these things, and the known laws of nature seem to exclude them. Because science can't accommodate or account for them, they do not happen.

The flaw in the argument is obvious enough: because there is so much evidence that paranormal events do happen – but not to order – it's clearly the laws of nature, as presently understood and stated, that are lacking. And such a mulish attitude is

Above: *Frederic W. Myers, one of the founders of the Society for Psychical Research. The aim of the SPR has always been to approach psychic phenomena in an objective, scientific spirit.*

Right: *The Yugoslav psychic Velibor undertakes a parapsychology experiment, monitored by the researcher who discovered him, Ainul Kebir. Velibor has succeeded many times in 'reading' letters and numbers contained in sealed envelopes.*

hardly fitting for a scientist, of all people – since the very basis of scientific endeavour is supposed to lie in the hope of discovering more about nature than we already know. In science laws are made to be broken; they are, as the old saw has it, for the guidance of wise men and the obedience of fools.

But investigations into the paranormal have always run up against one major difficulty and that is the notorious inconsistency of its effects. Telepathy, like other forms of extra-sensory perception (ESP), is no exception to this rule. Even very sensitive individuals don't receive information from other people's minds 100 per cent of the time, even when notably successful 'senders' are deliberately and carefully trying to transmit their thoughts to such a person. Nor do they always pick up the information with 100 per cent accuracy when they *do* receive it.

A good illustration of how blurred telepathic communication is can be had from the experience of George Gilbert Murray (1866–1957). In his day Murray was regarded as the world's greatest scholar of ancient Greek, but he also had a consistent and genuine telepathic talent, which he did his best to develop in 'guessing games' with his family. Murray did not limit himself to single objects, words or images on which someone else was concentrating: he could pick up entire quotations, episodes from public or family history, or scenes from books. In his study *The Paranormal* Dr Brian Inglis quotes what he calls a 'typical' example of one of Murray's successes, when the 'sender' was thinking of a scene in the French novel *Marie Claire*. Murray's response ran:

'This is a book – it's not English, not Russian – it's rather a – I think there are nuns in it – there are a lot of people – either a school or a laundry – and one of the nuns is weeping – I think it's French. Oh, it's a scene in *Marie Claire*, near the beginning – I can't remember it, but something like that – it's in the place where she goes – one of the nuns crying – a double name – no I can't get the – Marie Thérèse –.'

The name of the weeping nun in the scene from the book was in fact Marie Aimée. Whether that error was the result of Murray's memory of the book being at fault, or was a matter of garbled

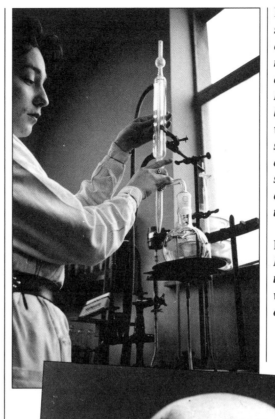

Left: *At the heart of the scientific method are experiments that can be repeated and verified by others, as in this laboratory. Psychical researchers have long attempted to make their work conform to this standard, although some object that this is no more sensible than trying to examine emotions in a test-tube.*

Below: *Professor Gilbert Murray, whose telepathic talents were tested and verified over decades of experiment.*

transmission, it is certainly typical of telepathy that even the best 'hits' are slightly awry.

And Murray did not have hits all the time, by any means. The results of some 50 years of his practice in these games were eventually published by the Society for Psychical Research, and they show that Murray was correct in only one-third of his 'guesses'. The other results included either failures in detail or attempts that did not work because guesses were simply not offered by Murray (another third), and the remaining third were ambiguous. Even so, such a high proportion of successes, especially given the elaborate kinds of target ideas that Murray was trying to pick up, is way above what anyone could explain away as 'chance' or 'coincidence'.

Murray did not, by any means, always have to have some prior knowledge of the subject he was offered in order to pick it up – even when it might be something as obscure as a scene from a book. Dr Inglis quotes an instance of this, but notes another curious aspect of it. Murray's impression was partly formed by the way his daughter had pictured the scene when it was chosen as a target for him.

The particular target was a scene from a book by Alexandre Aksakov, in which children were being taken by their parents to visit their grandparents. Murray did not identify the author, but he got the gist of the scene correctly – and added that the family was, he thought, crossing the River Volga. In the particular scene in question, they were not, but that image *had* been in his daughter's mind when the target was chosen, and does feature frequently in the book. The only explanation Murray could provide for this was, simply, that he had read his daughter's mind – in other words, it was her thoughts about the target that he had picked up, not the target itself.

MENTAL BLOCKAGE

Experiments in telepathy in the industrialized West are one thing; but some peoples living in constant and intimate contact with nature – and not in any sickly, patronizingly romantic sense, but through the sheer necessity of survival – seem to take telepathic communication for granted. This suggests that all of us may well have a telepathic ability, but that the ingrained habits of mind encouraged in industrialized societies – habits of will, of conscious, logical thinking rather than lateral or intuitive thinking – make it more difficult to get access to that ability.

Some specific instances of the *normality* of telepathic powers in traditional societies, as recorded by surprised Westerners, may serve to illustrate the difference between the two ways of looking at the world – and may illuminate the nature of the West's mental blockage when it comes to telepathy and associated forms of ESP.

HYPNOTIC DRUMS

In April 1962, the London *Times* carried a report of a bizarre telepathic relationship between an African family in the remote Singida province of Tanganyika (now Tanzania) and the local lion community. The family's ability to control lions was well known in the district, and villagers began to protest when the number of livestock killed by lions – but shared with them by their human controllers – reached new heights.

Colonel Mervin Cowie, the director of Kenya's national parks, told *The Times*: 'Recently one of the "lion-controllers" was gaoled by a chief after villagers protested…The man told the chief that unless he was freed by nightfall he would get his lions to kill the chief's cattle. The chief refused. Next morning fourteen of his cattle lay dead.'

FOOLISHLY THE CHIEF REFUSED TO FREE THE MAN WHO COULD CONTROL LIONS; WHEN THE DAWN CAME, THERE WERE FOURTEEN FRESHLY KILLED CATTLE CORPSES IN THE AFRICAN VILLAGE.

Below: *A Russian village on the banks of the River Volga, in Russia, which featured in a key experiment by Gilbert Murray.*

In his memoir *Africa Drums*, published in the 1930s, Richard St Barbe Baker, a conservator of forests in Kenya and in Nigeria during the early years of the 20th century, recalled a number of occasions when Kenyan tribesmen appeared to have received telepathic communications. For example, Baker describes how he was on a field trip in the foothills around Mount Kenya and around noon one day pitched camp. He continues:

'Lunch was served by a boy, who observed that Bwana Katchiku had died, this man being a well-respected farmer who lived some two hundred and fifty miles from the camp. When asked how he knew, the boy replied that N'degwa, one of the elders of the tribe about sixty years old, had "seen" it. He sent for the older man…

'"What is this? [Baker asked the elder when he arrived] Bwana Katchiku dead, you say? How did you learn of this?"

'"*N'iona*, I see it," was his astonishing reply.

'"When?" I demanded.

'"Now," he said. Somehow I knew he was speaking the truth, nor was there any reason for him to do otherwise.

'"I am sorry," I told him. "It is too bad…"

'"Yes, that is so," agreed N'degwa. "It is a bad business."

'N'degwa retired, but I made a mental note of the time and place. I pondered on the word *N'iona* – I see – which could not possibly be confounded with *S'kia* – I hear.

Left: *Kenyan warriors, like those who demonstrated extraordinary powers of clairvoyance to forester Richard St Barbe Baker. To the Africans, there was nothing unusual about their ability to see distant events in their minds.*

Below: *The Reading Jazz and Blues Festival in full swing in 1971. The power of music both to lull and stimulate at the same time creates a liberated state of mind similar to that created by hypnosis – which, it seems, brings out latent psychic powers.*

Above: *Laurens van der Post, who noted many instances of psychic communication among the San (Bushmen) of the Kalahari desert.*

THE OLD BUSHMAN KNEW THAT PEOPLE WERE HEADED IN THEIR DIRECTION – AND THAT THEY WERE IN TROUBLE.

'Seven days later a runner arrived at my camp with the news that Bwana Katchiku had died, at a distance of two hundred and fifty miles from camp.'

Note that Baker challenges (in best logical, Western fashion) the old man, as if he expects him to be lying, or to have *heard* the news, not seen it directly. But, as he admits, it became clear that the news had not already arrived; N'degwa had not heard about the farmer's death from a messenger of any kind. And in time, Baker came to accept this faculty among the native Kenyans, and even speculated that the hypnotic effect of drums released the ability to transmit and receive messages by mental energy alone.

This may not be the only stimulus that induces telepathic abilities. Baker himself also came to believe that Western people had lost the facility to practise telepathy because in the West 'the rhythm of life was conspicuous by its absence' and 'an air of worry and anxiety in competition' had replaced 'the serenity of the forest or wayside market'. But the paradoxical combination of simultaneous exhilaration,

relaxation, and well-being that music can so famously induce (witness the recurrent hysteria about rock'n'roll, which threatens almost everything the constipated Western mind has erected like a moat about its wilful consciousness) is not dissimilar from the peculiar state of swooning alertness that is typical of hypnotic trance, or the blissful awareness that meditation can bring.

MYSTERIOUS MUSICAL POWERS

Psychical researcher Joe Cooper, discussing Baker's African experiences in his book *Telepathy*, refers to the similarity between the effect of prolonged drumming and what he calls the *concentration* of hypnosis, and a resulting state of 'mental assonance'; but this is surely wrong. The drumming may have been concentrated, but its effect is surely different. It is the conscious, thinking, dominating mind that concentrates – and makes a bad hypnotic subject (and an awkward dancer). Whereas it is the unconscious, relaxed, accepting mind that achieves assonance (that is, harmony – a musical term!) with the world about it, which does not exclude either music or other human minds.

Cooper is probably wrong too in ascribing another Kenyan 'vision' that Baker witnessed to precognition. The instance was as follows, in Baker's words:

'I had a headman called N'duma. For my entertainment he had arranged for an evening with the drums. Two young men... incessantly played on their drums for about a couple of hours until even I became almost hypnotized with the monotony.

'Suddenly N'duma exclaimed, "Master, I see you are going for a journey. You are going up to my country. You are going to Meru."

'At that time I had no intention of going to Meru. It was out of my district and there was, as far as I knew, absolutely nothing to take me there.

'"What makes you say that, N'duma?" I asked.

'"*N'iona,*" was the reply, meaning simply, "I see it."'

A week later, Baker received orders to travel to Meru, which was some 200 miles from his station at the time. Cooper's – and Baker's – interpretation is that the headman was 'seeing' a future journey: but it seems more likely that N'duma was actually telepathically aware of the order being made, not the future event.

Another Western veteran of Africa, Laurens van der Post, has equally extraordinary stories to tell of the almost casual fashion in which the Bushmen of the Kalahari – a people whom he especially knows, loves and respects – treat telepathic experiences. In *The Heart of the Hunter*, Van der Post recounts how in the midst of an utterly silent, midday desert an old Bushman suddenly announced that there were people coming their way. There was no sign of any such thing, but the Bushman – and his interpreter, too – insisted that they could 'feel them coming here' (tapping at their chests), and that they were in trouble. And so it turned out to be. Van der Post's group gave the famished group food and water, and helped them on their way.

Another instance involved nothing more dramatic than an ostrich approaching: but the Bushman who became aware of the bird, while it was still out of sight, was also aware (because he felt the same sensation

in his own body) that the creature was scratching the back of its neck with its foot. This echoes another African who commented, sensing the presence of a zebra, that he knew it was nearby because 'I feel his stripes on my back' – such was his empathy with the animal.

It is perhaps worth noting – in view of both Richard St Barbe Baker's comments on the significance of drum music among the Kenyan tribesmen he worked with, and the still more obvious fear that 'primitive'

Van der Post cites instances of San people not merely seeing but identifying with approaching animals such as ostriches (below) and zebras (above), although the creatures were invisible to the physical eye. One told Van der Post that he knew a zebra was nearby because he could 'feel his stripes on my back'.

This was for youth, Strength, Mirth, and wit that Time
Most count their golden Age: but t'was not thine.
Thine was thy later yeares, so much refind
From youths Droſſe, Mirth, & wit; as thy pure mind
Thought (like the Angels) nothing but the Praiſe
Of thy Creator, in thoſe laſt, beſt Dayes.
Witnes this Booke, (thy Embleme) which begins
With Love; but endes, with Sighes, & Teares for ſins

IZ:WA:

Will: Marshall ſculpsit.

Above: *The frontispiece of John Donne's poems, published in 1649. In 1610, Donne had a disturbing and entirely accurate vision of his wife and their stillborn child.*

HER HAIR WAS HANGING AROUND HER SHOULDERS AND A DEAD CHILD LAY IN HER ARMS.

---

the human reflection of both the stately and the intimate rhythms of nature – bring out the latent psychic abilities of humankind? It is a question that those who have organized the crude and impersonal guessing games that have so long passed for 'research' in telepathy might do well to address.

EXCRUCIATING PAIN

While laboratory research into telepathy has failed to prove the existence of ESP to the satisfaction of scientists – and has even involved fraud on a few occasions – everyday experience of telepathy by ordinary people persists in defying rational explanation and continues to provide the most convincing evidence that such a

music like rock'n'roll (which has many African characteristics) generates in certain orthodox Western minds – what Van der Post has to say about the place of music among the Bushmen (who, he was surprised to find, had no drums) in his book *The Lost World of the Kalahari*:

'Music was as vital as water, food, and fire to them, for we never found a group so poor or desperate that they did not have some musical instrument with them. And all their music, song, sense of rhythm, and movement achieved its greatest expression in their dancing. They passed their days and nights with purpose and energy, but dancing too played the same deep part in their lives, as [it did for] the Bushmen of old in legend and history.'

Does the liberating effect of music and a nearness to the subtleties of the natural world – and music, after all, is no more than

faculty does indeed exist. And accounts of telepathy go back a very long way.

The English poet and cleric John Donne (1572–1631) was not, perhaps, an ordinary man, but a genius for poetry does not necessarily imply any predisposition toward psychic talents. In his biography of Donne, Sir Izaak Walton recounts that in 1610 or so the poet (who was also a courtier) was sent to France on a diplomatic mission; his wife remained at home, since she was pregnant. When Sir Robert Drury, the English ambassador in Paris, went to meet Donne, he found him 'so altered as to his looks as amazed Sir Robert to behold him'.

Donne finally managed to account for his condition. 'I have seen a dreadful vision,' he explained. 'I have seen my dear wife pass twice by me through this room, with her hair hanging about her shoulders, and a dead child in her arms.'

Drury reluctantly agreed to send a messenger to England to discover what, if anything, was ailing Donne's wife. Twelve days later, the man returned to report that he had found Mrs Donne, as Walton put it, 'very sad, and sick in her bed; and that after a long and dangerous labour, she had been delivered of a dead child. And, upon examination, the abortion proved to be the same day, and about the very hour, that Mr Donne affirmed he saw her pass by him in his chamber.'

As with precognition, and as we noted above, telepathy seems most often to occur spontaneously as a reaction to a crisis, but

Below: *Scene in the Lake District, where Arthur Severn had an accident experienced by his wife.*

Above: *Building the Blue Nile dam in the Sudan in the 1920s. Such projects are typical of the Western tendency to manipulate and control the natural world, rather than harmonize with it. Such a domineering outlook suppresses natural psychic powers – and is usually disastrous for the environment, too.*

it remains unfathomable why a particular individual should telepathically 'tune in' to a particular crisis and not another. In the cases of Cassirer and Donne, both picked up some kind of signal from people with whom they had very strong emotional bonds, and at very critical times. But it seems hardly likely that the following instances of telepathically transmitted pain were the greatest emotional or physical crises suffered by the two couples involved.

Joan R. Severn, wife of the distinguished English landscape painter Arthur Severn, recounted to the art critic John Ruskin how, at about 7 am one summer morning in 1880, she woke up with a start, 'feeling I had had a hard blow on my mouth, and with a distinct sense that I had been cut and was bleeding under my upper lip, [I] seized my pocket handkerchief and held it...to the part...after a few seconds, when I removed it, I was astonished not to see any blood, and only then realized it was impossible anything could have struck me there, as I lay fast asleep in bed, and so I thought it was only a dream!'

Joan Severn noted the time, noticed too that her husband was not there and assumed he had gone out sailing – the Severns lived near Coniston Water, in the Lake District of Westmorland – and went back to sleep. About two and a half hours later, Severn came back from the lake for breakfast, and kept dabbing at his lip. Eventually he admitted that he had run into a squall while on the water: trying to get out of the way of the boat's suddenly swinging boom, he had had a sound crack across the mouth from the tiller. He had not been wearing a watch, but when his wife told him of her own sudden and painful awakening, calculated that the accident would have happened at about the same time as she started awake.

In 1947, Leslie Boughey was stationed with the RAF at El-Firdan in Egypt. He and his wife wrote to each other every day – she was in England, working in a factory near Stoke-on-Trent. He wrote to her one day telling how he had woken up in the night with 'the most excruciating pain' in one hand, and particularly in one finger. 'There was no mark on my finger, no swelling, inflammation, or anything, yet I just wanted to hold it and scream,' Boughey told researchers for the TV series *Arthur C. Clarke's World of Mysterious Powers*. Eventually, after a few hours of sweating and suffering, the agony subsided.

Boughey's letter telling his wife about this mysterious attack crossed in the mail with a letter from her. At work, she said, a fragment of metal had penetrated her finger, and the wound had turned septic. She had gone to the doctor, who had lanced the infected part. 'The extraordinary thing was,' said Boughey, 'the time of her operation coincided exactly with my painful experience: the same hand, even the same finger.'

TELEPATHIC TRAP

Telepathy, for some reason, is fickle: communicating quite trivial crises with excruciating force, and major ones with no more than a sudden pang of anxiety. And it is fickle too in its choice of subjects. It is not always people who have a close relationship or strong emotional ties who find themselves in touch by 'mental radio'.

Early one morning in 1980, 81-year-old Isabella Casas made her way slowly into her local police station in Barcelona, and stammered out a bizarre story to the officers there. She had just awoken from an appalling dream in which she had seen the face of her neighbour, Rafael Perez, 'twisted in terror', as she heard his voice saying, 'They are going to kill us.'

What stopped the police dismissing the nightmarish vision as merely a bad dream was Sra Casas's further concern. Perez, a 56-year-old chef, would normally visit her every day – but he had not called for ten days. Even odder, she had had a note from him – delivered by hand – three days *after* she had last seen him, which said he would be away for several weeks. Why had he not called to tell her in person? The police decided to start a search for Perez.

They found him tied up in a utility room on the roof of his and Sra Casas's own apartment house. He had been hidden there by two men who had broken into his flat, forced him to sign 28 bank cheques so that they could withdraw his $30,000-worth of savings without being noticed, and made him write the note to Sra Casas to allay her suspicions before tying him up. When they had all the money, they said, they would return and kill him and the old lady. The

Below: *A successful experiment in parapsychology. The typewritten 'target' phrase was hidden in a sealed box but was nevertheless accurately read by 15-year-old Monica Nieto Tejada in 1989.*

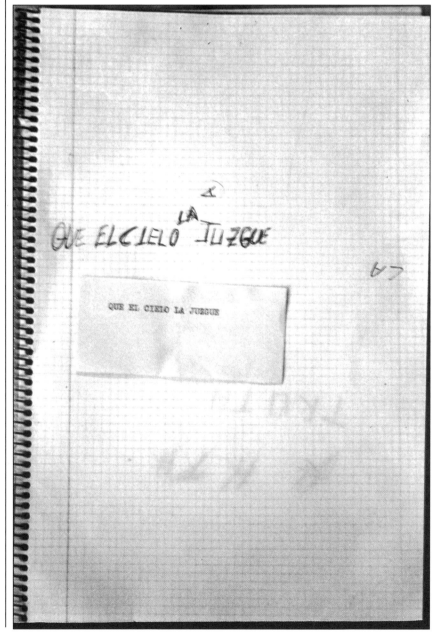

Right: *Teenage Spanish psychic Monica Nieto Tejada with experimenter Dr Elmar Gruber and another successful 'hit' achieved by extra-sensory perception.*

police simply waited for the two criminals to return, trapped them and arrested them.

THE BATTLE AGAINST NATURE

But why are these cases so rare, and why is telepathy so incomplete in the West, yet precise and part of the ordinary fabric of life for, say, an African Bushman?

To put it at its simplest, the great division between the modern Western outlook and that of traditional societies is this. The Western mind seeks to dominate the environment: it sees a plot of land, for instance, as something to exploit – to settle, to build hotels on, to bend to its will. It doesn't matter if this involves damming rivers, dredging harbours, razing forests and destroying wildlife. Success is measured by the extent to which things have been changed to suit the whim of human beings. At its worst, the Western mind treats the environment as an enemy.

The traditional way of looking at things is, on the other hand, passive: it seeks to absorb knowledge of the place, so that life – that is, the means of survival – can *fit in* with what already exists. Bridges may still be built, animals killed, the land tilled: but the traditional mind sees the natural world as something to listen to and co-operate with in order to make survival easier, not something to defeat.

The difference between the modern Western cast of mind and that of traditional societies is in essence the difference between confrontation with the environment and persuasion and compromise with it.

This tendency of the Western mind to see things in terms of black or white only, to see life as a series of oppositions and challenges and potential duels, may explain why laboratory experiments in telepathy and other forms of extra-sensory perception so often fail in the West, and fail in particular in the presence of sceptics. This phenomenon, known as the 'sheep/goat effect', has been noted many times by parapsychologists. A sheep, or believer in ESP, will get better results in ESP experiments than a goat, or sceptic – whether the sheep or goat is being tested *or is actually the person conducting the tests.*

In any case the notion of coldly testing for ESP in a laboratory is, in effect, a challenge, an implicit contest, in which one side or the other will 'win'. It is not an invitation to demonstrate a certain ability, but an obstacle to be overcome.

But in societies that keep the seemingly inevitable, perhaps inherent human propensity for competitiveness within carefully defined bounds – instead of making it a principle of 'good' conduct – and that have a relaxed, accepting outlook upon the natural world, psychic powers seem to flourish, along with other arts. And this is not wishful thinking. There is a wealth of historical and anthropological evidence that the most adept psychics within a tribe or community would certainly be regarded as unusual, but they would not be ostracized or even mocked. They would certainly not be ignored: it is more likely they would be revered. Such individuals`might become a *shaman* or a medicine man – a '*witch doctor*' in crude colonialist terms, but actually the role is nearer that of priest, wise man, and tribal counsellor, rolled into one.

In the same way, the most talented poets or musicians would be recognized and elevated to a privileged position. Even in the West such 'acceptable' kinds of visionary still are so rewarded, if often grudgingly, since even the Western mind cannot bring itself wholly to deny the life of the spirit.

Western science, the epitome of logic and calculated thinking, cannot accommodate the life of the spirit, because it cannot measure it – or master it. Therefore it excludes it. While scientific thinking has come insidiously to dominate our lives, so that most people unconsciously assume that what cannot be proven by science cannot be taken entirely seriously, there are still eruptions of art, music and paranormal events to remind us that science's view of life may be powerful, but it is neither wholly true nor truly whole.

Below: *Medium Marvello Creti and members of his Societa Ergoniana. Creti was hailed as one of Italy's greatest inventors in the 1930s, but turned from material to spiritual interests. Today the society's base, a 16th-century former monastery near Sutri, contains machinery built by Creti to 'influence energy' in the human body.*

SLIPS IN TIME

Lost in foul weather and piloting a poorly equipped plane, Victor Goddard knew that his life depended on him finding the right direction. What he didn't expect to do was to fly into the future...

In 1934, Victor Goddard (later Air Marshal Sir Victor Goddard) of the Royal New Zealand Air Force had to fly a Hawker Hart biplane bomber from Scotland to England. On the way, he ran into bad weather and then had the nasty experience of going into a tailspin. After getting out of that scrape, he realized he was no longer sure where he was. The aircraft lacked sophisticated instruments and he was navigating by sight – and in that weather there was not much to be seen.

Goddard knew he ought to be within a few miles of Drem, an airfield that had been in use in World War 1 but had since been abandoned. Not long before, he had actually visited the place by car, just to find out if it was still possible to land there. He had found instead that the airstrip had been turned over to farmland, and that the former hangars were now being used as barns. But from the air he would certainly recognize Drem, and if he could find it, he could get himself back on course. Goddard lost height, flew under the cloud, and went to look for the disused airfield.

He found it. The first odd thing about the place was that it was bathed in sunlight, despite the inclement weather he had just encountered. Still more surprising – despite what he had seen just a few days previously – the airfield was now fully operational. The hangars had been repaired, and on the freshly laid tarmac apron sat four aircraft – one of them a monoplane fighter of a type he had never seen before. The final touch of strangeness was that these aircraft were painted yellow, and the ground crew around them were wearing blue uniforms.

It was weird enough to find an abandoned airfield suddenly in tip-top working order, but there were no aircraft in the RAF painted yellow, and in any case all RAF fighters in service at that time were biplanes: the first monoplane, the Hurricane, did not even fly until 1935. And RAF technicians wore khaki denim uniforms. What had suddenly happened at Drem? The place was real enough: Goddard took new bearings and completed his flight safely.

Reporting what he had seen to his wing commander, he was told unhelpfully but unambiguously to 'lay off the Scotch'. In 1938, Drem was reopened as a flight training station. By then, the first Hurricanes were entering RAF service, and training aircraft were routinely painted yellow to distinguish them from operational aircraft. Ground crew, too, were issued new working uniforms – denims in a dark shade of RAF blue. When

The RAF's first monoplane fighter was the formidable Hawker Hurricane (opposite), which entered service in 1935. Yet on a flight in 1934, Victor Goddard flew over an airfield where he saw not only a Hurricane, but one mysteriously painted yellow. He and his aircraft seemed somehow to have slipped forward in time.

Below: *RAF station officers – practical men like Victor Goddard, who had a timeslip in 1934.*

he eventually discovered and put together all these bits of the jigsaw, Goddard realized that he had seen Drem not as it actually was on that intemperate day in 1934, but as it was to be in the not too distant future. He had even managed to slip in time to a day when the weather was fine – helping him find his way home.

Below: *In 1973, a Norfolk coin collector got a genuinely old-fashioned look from a shop assistant when he handed her a 5p piece – one of the decimal coins issued in 1971 and shown here – for he had, it seems, stepped back into the Edwardian era, when there were 20 shillings and 240 pence to the £1 sterling.*

Goddard seems to have been a man with a charmed life when it came to narrow shaves in aircraft – later in his career he escaped a crash landing that should have devastated the aircraft he was in, and that he had been forewarned would result in his death. But there is a key difference between the premonitory vision that warned Goddard of that crash and what he experienced directly in 1934. For the premonitory vision was just that: a mental image of the future. In this case, Goddard – and his aircraft! – actually seem to have shifted, both together, from a foul-weather day in 1934 to a fair-weather day sometime after 1938. Goddard had experienced what psychical researchers call a timeslip.

TIME TRAVELLER

Goddard's experience was relatively unusual – but by no means unique – in being a slip *forward* in time. It is, for some reason, more common for those who have been subjected to timeslips to find themselves walking into the past. Joan Forman, who has researched and described a formidable range of these experiences (and on whose work any discussion of the phenomenon must rely very heavily), reported in her book *The Mask of Time* the intriguing case of an elderly man she called Mr Squirrel – who, like Goddard, slipped across time in pursuit of a particular personal need.

Squirrel was an enthusiastic amateur numismatist, a coin-collector, from Norfolk, England. Sometime in 1973 he found he needed some envelopes in which to store his coins, and he went to nearby Great Yarmouth, a resort on the coast, to find some. He had heard that there was a stationer's shop there that stocked exactly the thing he needed. Squirrel had never been to the shop before, but he did know how to reach it.

When he got there, he noticed that the street was still laid in old-fashioned cobbles, but that the shop itself looked bright, new, and freshly painted. When he went into the shop he found it empty, and glanced around at the place: the till was an old-fashioned box type; there was a frame full of walking-sticks for sale; decorated frames for photographs were on display. Then a young assistant approached him, wearing a long black skirt and a blouse with 'mutton-chop' sleeves; her hair was piled on top of her head.

Squirrel told her what he wanted, and she produced a brown box full of small, transparent envelopes. He commented that they had a surprising amount in stock. The girl explained that fishermen bought them all the time, to keep hooks in. She told him the price of his purchases was a shilling: he gave her a new 5p piece, which was then the same size, colour, weight and – most important – the same value as the old shilling coin. Then he left the shop. All the time he had been in it, there was no sound from outside and inside there had been absolute quiet apart from his conversation with the girl.

Squirrel thought little of these details at the time: many girls were wearing clothes with a Victorian or Edwardian flavour in 1973, and doing their hair to match; decimal coinage had been introduced only two years before, and he (like many people, especially the elderly) still thought of prices in the old money. The shop assistant apparently looked at the coin he gave her with some surprise, although she said nothing about it. However, the details of that visit did come to mind with some force when Squirrel went back to the shop a week later for more envelopes for his coin collection.

This time, there were no cobbles in the street, but ordinary modern paving stones.

The shop façade now looked weathered, not bright. Inside, too, the details had changed. The mature lady who served him denied any knowledge of a young girl assistant, and then said the shop not only had none of the envelopes Squirrel wanted – but had never stocked them!

This experience would have been uncanny enough; what makes it especially so was the fact that Squirrel still had the envelopes that he had bought in his brief visit to another age – and could not have bought them in 1973. Joan Forman tracked down their makers, who confirmed that they were sold in the 1920s, although they were first made before 1914.

Without the envelopes, it is reasonable to suggest that the elderly Mr Squirrel's experience, on its own, had been some kind of hallucination, or at any rate a purely mental journey across time. However, it is not possible to describe the set of new transparent envelopes that followed Squirrel back into 1973 as some kind of portable phantasm. This disconcerting detail raises even more questions about the nature of timeslips than does the apparent ability of Victor Goddard's very solid aircraft to travel with him into the future.

GHOSTLY MONKS

Two other intriguing instances reported by Joan Forman show a quite different facet of this mysterious phenomenon – and give yet another twist to the problem of what actually happens in a timeslip. Both timeslips happened to the same person, a Mrs Turrell-Clarke, who experienced them when she was living in the quaintly named village of Wisley-cum-Pyrford in Surrey. And both suggest that her timeslips, at least, were indeed a journey of the mind, or possibly even of the soul.

In the first of these strange events, Mrs Turrell-Clarke was cycling from her home to the village church, where she was going to the evensong service. Suddenly, the modern road under her turned into a path across a field; her bicycle vanished; and she found herself on foot. Approaching her was a man dressed like a 13th-century peasant. She herself, she felt, was wearing a nun's habit. The man stood aside to let her go by. Within seconds the scene shifted again, and the mystified Mrs Turrell-Clarke found

herself back on her bicycle in the middle of the 20th century.

Her second experience came a month later. This time she was actually in the church at Pyrford at a service. She was joining in the singing of a plainsong chant when the church – which dates back to the 13th century – apparently regressed in front of her eyes to its original state. The floor was of plain earth, the altar of stone; and in the centre of the church a group of monks in brown habits were in procession, singing the same plainsong chant that Mrs Turrell-Clarke had joined in singing just a few minutes before – or, to put it another way, some 700 years later!

The most curious part of the experience, however, was that Mrs Turrell-Clarke felt that, during the few moments it lasted, she was viewing this scene as 'one of a small group of people at the back of the church, taking little part in the proceedings'.

Pyrford church was originally a chapel belonging to nearby Newark Abbey. The monks there wore black habits, but Mrs Turrell-Clarke discovered that in 1293 the monks of Westminster Abbey had used the chapel – and they wore brown habits. Presumably it was members of this order that she had seen; at least the information gave some credibility to her odd experience.

Above: *An Edwardian shop with the kind of fittings and decor that greeted the Norfolk numismatist in his timeslip in 1973.*

SHE WAS A MIGRANT FROM THE FUTURE, SUMMONED TO THE PAST BY THE CHANTS OF THE BROWN-ROBED MONKS.

But what kind of experience was it, really? Both these timeslips could be regarded as in some sense imaginary, however authentic the details. Yet if in both these cases Mrs Turrell-Clarke did slip through time for a few minutes, who was she, and where was she, while she visited the Surrey of the 13th century? Were these simply very elaborate forms of ghosts that she saw – phantoms of the Surrey landscape and the Pyrford church, complete with inhabitants?

This seems unlikely, for she saw these things through someone else's eyes. In her first timeslip, she felt she was wearing nun's robes. But who was the nun? Mrs Turrell-Clarke in a previous incarnation? An innocent religious whose consciousness was briefly taken over by this migrant from the future? Or was some kind of long-distance, time-travelling telepathy involved, so that she saw the past through someone else's mind, but without taking it over? And was she still seeing through the eyes of the nun in her second timeslip, or through another person's? And for what purpose did they occur? No special information was passed on to the witness; no problem was solved – far from it: every aspect of these cases bristles with problems.

However, an especially interesting question is raised by the possibility that these visions were telepathic in nature. Did the person, or people, through whom she

Below: The parish church at Wisley-cum-Pyrford, Surrey, where one involuntary time-traveller saw monks from an order based at Westminster Abbey (right), who used the church only during the 13th century.

had these experiences in turn see into the future, while she looked into the past? The question '*Where* was Mrs Turrell-Clarke during her timeslip?' becomes more and more intriguing – and more and more difficult to answer – if they did use her mind as a window onto times to come.

PHANTOM OMNIBUS

One interpretation of timeslips, as mentioned above, is that they are forms of haunting. If there is anything to this speculation, the 'ghosts' involved are not purely spirits, or spiritual representations, of dead people in the way we usually take ghosts to be. That spectres of inanimate objects do apparently exist is nothing new in the annals of psychical research: a famous example is the phantom No 7 omnibus belonging to London Transport that on various occasions in the 1930s was seen powering down Cambridge Gardens

in Notting Hill, causing at least one motorist to plough into parked cars in an attempt to avoid it.

Even if one accepts that a phantom path can haunt its descendant, a modern road, or that the past life of a church can cloak its modern interior, the timeslips experienced by Mr Squirrel and Mrs Turrell-Clarke were singular in that both the witnesses *interacted* with the so-called ghosts: a peasant stood to one side to let Mrs Turrell-Clarke go by; Mr Squirrel not only had a whole conversation with a phantom shop-girl in a phantom shop, he bought a set of phantom envelopes that nevertheless remained strikingly physical and material even when Squirrel himself had 'come out' of his timeslip.

The experience of Victor Goddard (and, as we shall see, others who have found themselves briefly inhabiting the future) also, rather comprehensively, disposes of the 'haunting' interpretation of timeslips. A complete collection of all the reports of hauntings from the future would make a very thin book indeed. The text would be something of an anticlimax, too. It would consist of three words: 'None so far.'

'GHOULE OF TOMORROW'

This does not mean that on his strange flight into the future Goddard and his aircraft might not have seemed spectral to anyone on the ground, had they bothered to look up. And perhaps a 13th-century Surrey peasant went home one night to tell the story of the nun he had seen unexpectedly appear on the path, and stood aside for, and seen vanish before his eyes…

Something like this may be reported in the distant future by a family living in what is now Germany. In the early 1980s a British family was travelling on one of the former West Germany's autobahns. The road wasn't busy, and their attention was taken by a lone vehicle approaching very

Below: *A London omnibus of the 1930s – like the one that occasionally haunted Cambridge Gardens in London's Notting Hill district.*

Are all ghosts spirits of the dead, or are some the spectres of living people caught in a timeslip? The driver of a ghostly Roman chariot (right) *may be as astonished to see us as we are to see him. A cross-haunting, or double timeslip, like this occurred between an 18th-century gentleman and healer Matthew Manning* (below) *when the latter was a teenager in the early 1970s.*

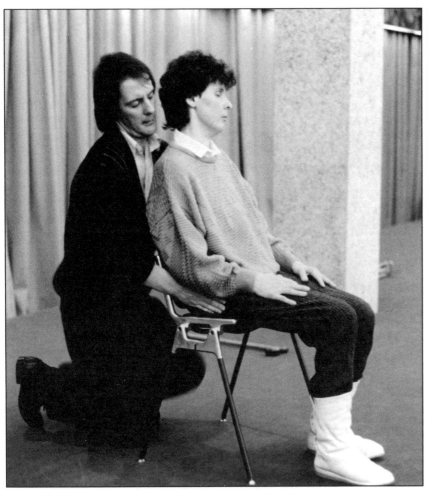

THE CAR WHICH HURTLED PAST THEM WAS A PHANTOM OF THE FUTURE, BUT ITS OCCUPANTS WERE FOUR VERY FRIGHTENED PEOPLE.

British family saw a phantom from the future, it was clear the phantoms were equally astonished and alarmed to be seeing a ghostly automobile from what to them was the distant past – no doubt a sight as disconcerting as that of a spectral Roman chariot rattling down a modern *autostrada* would be today.

The British healer and psychic Matthew Manning experienced a bizarre series of episodes in his adolescence that bears out the notion that if there is an interaction with figures from the past or future during a timeslip, the other party involved will see the present-day witness as some kind of 'ghost'.

In 1971 Manning met an apparition of a man, walking with the help of two sticks, on the stairs of his parents' house – which dated back to the 17th and 18th centuries. The ghost was no translucent spectre, however: it was apparently solid, and Manning at first took it to be a living man – not least because he spoke to him. Rather matter-of-factly the man apologized for alarming Manning, and explained that he was taking exercise for the sake of his legs, which were bothering him. The entity claimed to be one Robert Webbe, who had in fact owned the house and had parts of it built. It was then that Manning realized he had encountered a ghost.

Webbe appeared many times after that. The apparition became almost part of the family, even playing pranks on them. At other times Manning communicated with Webbe through automatic writing. At one point in such a dialogue he asked Webbe if

fast on the other side of the divided highway. It looked like no car they had ever seen – in fact it looked more like a UFO. It had no wheels visible, and was cylindrical in shape. There were four round porthole-like windows. As it flashed by, they saw four 'very frightened faces' staring at them out of the windows. If the

there were a ghost in the house. Webbe indignantly denied it: if there were, he would 'chase it away'. He added that he thought Manning was merely trying to frighten him.

Manning then asked Webbe whom he thought he was talking to. Webbe gave the following fascinating reply: 'I think sometimes I am going mad. I hear a voyce in myne head which I hear talking to me. But tell no one else they locke me away.'

Manning then explained why he was asking these questions. As far as he was concerned, he himself was in the here and now and solid flesh; Webbe, to him, was a ghost. At this, Webbe reportedly became distressed, and unable to believe what he was being told. He ended by insisting that Manning must be a 'ghoule of tomorrow'.

What seems to have happened in this case – especially given the notable solidity of Webbe's form, and his ability to have otherwise ordinary two-way conversations when he was actually visible – is a kind of *cross*-haunting – or a two-way timeslip. Both parties involved thought they were being haunted. It is as if two segments of time were interlocking – rather as if the circles of light from two spotlights were overlapping. But how this happens remains as mysterious as any other aspect of any other kind of timeslip.

STRANGE BLACKOUT

Timeslips may involve more than people and places. In at least two instances, they have featured radio transmissions from the distant past.

Alan Holmes, First Radio Officer of the Cunard liner *Queen Elizabeth 2*, was on watch in the radio shack aboard the ship during a transatlantic voyage some time in 1978, listening for messages on the frequency reserved for radio-telephone (RT) communications, when he received a message in Morse code: 'GKS GBTT QSX AREA 1A'.

There were several things wrong with this message. First, what was a Morse message doing on the RT voice frequency? Next, the message, once translated from Morse, was still using a code for ship-to-shore messages that had gone out of use years before. Third, the message appeared at first glance to be coming from the *QE2* herself, whose call sign is GBTT, or 'Golf Bravo Tango Tango'.

Holmes said: 'It was uncanny...The radio procedure used was dropped years ago...it came from another age. I can't believe it was sent by a ghost.'

If it was not a ghost, then the next most reasonable explanation seems to be that a timeslip had occurred. For the call sign

> **THE TIMID OLD GENTLEMAN WAS TERRIFIED OF BEING LOCKED UP IN A LUNATIC ASYLUM AND SO TOLD NO ONE ABOUT THE VOICES HE WAS HEARING.**

Below: *The* **Queen Elizabeth 2,** *which in 1978 received a radio message out of the past from its long-since retired fellow-Cunarder* **Queen Mary.**

Above: *The liner* **Queen Mary,** *the apparent sender of a radio message that was not picked up until at least 11 years after its transmission.*

GBTT was also used by the old Cunarder *Queen Mary* – and she had been taken out of service in 1967, and sold to the City of Long Beach, California, where she was turned into a floating hotel and conference centre. And the form of the transmission was exactly the one that was in use when the *Queen Mary* was at sea. Holmes deciphered the anachronistic message as a routine position check from the old liner *Queen Mary* to the international shipping radio station Portishead, which is at Burnham in Somerset.

It's coincidence enough that the *QE2* had inherited the call sign from the *Queen Mary* before the code was discontinued; it is quite bizarre that the new ship, with that same call sign, should have picked up a message sent out at least 11 years previously.

Holmes suggested an explanation: 'Sometimes radio signals bounce off the moon and "turn up" in Australia. This message could have bounced out into space more than ten years ago and just zipped around until it found its way back to Earth

and we picked it up.' He suggested that the signal might have bounced off something at least five light years away in space and, by an extraordinary freak, come back to Earth in such a way that the *QE2* had been in the way of the returning signal. The odds against that happening are, however, literally astronomical or 'inconceivable', as a spokesman for Portishead put it.

When Donald Mulholland, the station manager for Portishead, was interviewed about the affair in the Autumn 1978 edition of *Hello World*, the magazine of the Post Office External Telecommunications Executive, he suggested that the whole thing was a hoax. Holmes retorted by saying he was fed up with justifying the event: 'If I'd been alone on watch, I'd never have mentioned it. I was not alone in the radio shack at the time, and the message really did come in.' If it was a hoax, he went on, it would be difficult to lay on and hardly worth the bother. 'The hoaxer would have had to know exactly what frequency we were listening out on and when.'

BBC TV's report on 11 August 1978 about the bizarre message revealed a further curious detail: shortly after the *QE2* received the message, 'a mysterious blackout silenced all messages to and from Atlantic shipping for a time'.

Another strange case of a timeslipping radio message was also reported in 1978. After Mrs Helen Griffith wrote to the London *Daily Express* describing how she had heard the sounds of a World War 2 battle as she crossed the English Channel in 1977, a Mr A.J. Peterson wrote to the newspaper in response (the letter was printed in the 22 August editions), with another story of an inexplicable radio message that had somehow slipped in time. While his son was serving with the Green Howards in Borneo in 1968, his patrol picked up a radio message they couldn't decipher. 'Back at base they handed the message to intelligence who found that it was in a long-discarded code…[It turned out to be] a message sent during an action in the last war.'

ECHOES OF THE PAST

The sounds of battle are sometimes heard again years after the event. The most famous such case is that of two women who, while on holiday in Puys, near Dieppe, on 4 August 1951, claimed to have heard a blow-by-blow re-run of the assault on Dieppe by an Allied amphibious force on 19 August 1942. That battle left 3623 killed or wounded. The ladies' account seemed to tally with the military records, and investigators for the Society for Psychical Research stated their belief that it was 'a genuine psychic experience'. But whether this was a timeslip, a mass phantom, or a simple delusion, is open to question. It has also come to light that the ladies' oft-cited claim to have known nothing about the military details of the Dieppe raid may well be false.

The most recent such account maintains that sounds from World War 2 sea battles can still be heard echoing around the North Atlantic. The US Navy has a network of super-sensitive hydrophones called SOSUS (Sound Surveillance System) buried on the ocean floor to detect enemy submarine traffic. Armies of listeners compare the incoming sounds with vast computerized libraries of natural sounds and the known engine noises ('sound signatures') of vessels in the world's submarine navies. According to the magazine *US News and World Report*, sounds like distant explosions and cannon fire have been picked up ever since SOSUS was installed in 1952.

It has been suggested that the sounds were perpetuated by freak conditions that made the sea act like a superconductor. One expert in underwater surveillance thought the cause might be deep undersea channels, which do indeed exist, that 'act like huge natural telephone cables. Sound seems to be able to travel along them without deterioration in the signal. The sound goes back and forth, losing hardly any of its strength.' But, he said, 'not all sounds are "stored" in this way for years. The sounds apparently have to have occurred at the right place…but how [they] get into this system remains a mystery.'

Some apparent timeslips may, then, have a natural explanation, but most, it is absolutely clear, do not. The answer to the mysteries they present is buried somewhere in the extraordinary, and barely understood, capacities of the human mind.

THE RECEIVER PICKED UP THE MESSAGE ACCURATELY – BUT IT WAS A MESSAGE FROM ANOTHER TIME.

Below: *British troops returning from the disastrous raid on enemy-occupied Dieppe in 1942. Nine years later, two English ladies on holiday nearby claimed they heard a replay of the battle.*

MIND OVER MATTER

Uri Geller seemed to prove the power of the mind over matter. Many set out to expose him as a fraud, and as the tests became more and more difficult, it seemed that Geller was bound to fail...

Probably the world's best-known exponent of the mind's power over matter is the Israeli psychic Uri Geller. As a result of the international attention that the media gave Geller in the early 1970s, hundreds of thousands, possibly millions, of people around the world became aware of the phenomenon of psychokinesis – the ability of the mind to affect material objects in unexpected ways.

Geller bent spoons under the glare of TV camera lights merely by stroking them; at his word, clocks and watches that had been put away as useless began ticking again; scientists watched him make Geiger counters go haywire and sail through standard ESP tests without a hitch. On one especially celebrated occasion he took a spoon from the Marquess of Bath's priceless gold cutlery service and made it fall in two pieces with hardly any visible physical effort – again, in full view of TV cameras.

Whatever the merits of Geller's claims to fame – and there has been a horde of noisy sceptics vociferously claiming that he is a fraud, and that they know how he does his tricks, pursuing Geller ever since he came to international attention – perhaps the best way to put any claim to psycho-kinetic powers is in its proper context.

SCEPTICS

To begin with, Geller's claims are by no means new. Many others before him have said that they can influence material things by mental powers alone and, without pretending that they understand how they can do so, have convinced trained, observ-

ant, and by no means gullible witnesses that they were indeed capable of just that. Some justified their abilities by ascribing them to the intervention of spirits; others offered no explanation at all, but the effects occurred nonetheless.

An even more important point about psychokinesis is that it is no more than an *extension* of the known ability of the mind. While almost all of Geller's predecessors in the history of psychokinesis have been attacked as fraudulent, sceptics have conveniently overlooked the fact that every day of their lives they themselves employ a faculty for 'mind over matter' – as do the rest of us, even people who have never heard of psychokinesis and could not care less about it.

Consider what happens when we feel thirsty. We get up and walk toward the nearest tap or we make for the nearest bar, or we brew a cup of tea. Similarly, what happens when we see the cat heading with remorseless determination toward our dinner of cold chicken that we left on the table while we answered the phone? We

Above: *Uri Geller performs an experiment in psychokinesis live on TV in Luxembourg. Geller has never shrunk from scientific investigation of his powers.*

Opposite: *Geller bends a key merely by holding it in one hand and concentrating on it, in a demonstration on Danish TV in January 1974.*

Right: *Others besides Geller have shown many times that psychokinetic metal-bending is possible. These objects were distorted in various experiments held in Europe and supervised by Dr Elmar Gruber between 1976 and 1982.*

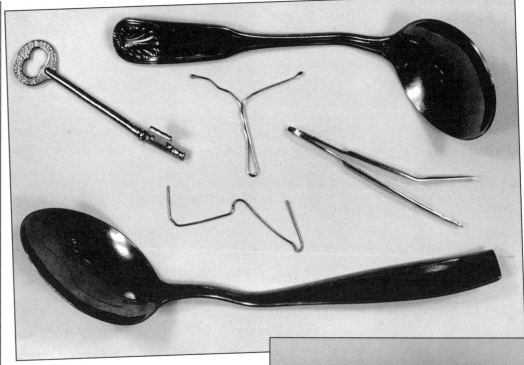

shoo it off, very quickly. What made the cat head inexorably for our chicken drumsticks in the first place?

The answer is simply that the cat is acting on the *idea* that those pieces of chicken would be very tasty indeed, thank you. Similarly the *idea* of wanting to slake our thirst drives us to a drink of some kind, and the *idea* that the cat not only does not deserve the dinner we have prepared for ourselves, but may well choke on splinters of bone, drives us to chase it away from the table. Mind influences matter every day, indeed every minute, of our lives. If it did not, sceptics of psychokinesis would not even be able to get out of bed of a morning, and certainly could not open their mouths to cry 'Fraud!' at the tops of their voices.

DOUBLE-TALK

The relentlessly materialist drift of modern science has gone so far as to deny this fundamental interaction between mind and matter. Some biologists would even deny the existence of human or animal consciousness on the grounds that it cannot be detected by instruments. The question of how they could reach such a ludicrous conclusion *without* a consciousness of some kind with which to think never seems to have crossed their minds – despite the obvious brevity of the journey demanded by the thought.

In his book *Knowing and Being*, philosopher and scientist Michael Polanyi quotes a number of neurologists on this point – among them Drs Hebb and Kubie. The former stated that 'The existence of something called consciousness is a venerable *hypothesis*: not a datum, not directly observable', while Kubie pronounced that 'Although we cannot get along without the concept of consciousness, actually there is no such thing.'

'Examples,' says Polanyi, 'of such double-talk and double-think could be multiplied from the whole range of biological sciences.' He brilliantly illustrates this obtuseness of the materialist view in his description of an episode that occurred at the annual meeting of the American Association for the Advancement of Science in December 1956. Polanyi had urged that gathering in New York to 'recognize the absurdity of regarding human beings as insentient automata'. Polanyi said he could not believe his ears at the response: 'The distinguished neurologist, R.W. Gerard, answered me passionately: "One thing we do know, ideas don't move muscles!"'

Polanyi's own view was encapsulated in his pithy aphorism: 'The mind is the body's meaning.' But when people live daily with the contradictions and constraints of a discipline that demands that they deny their own ability to move their own muscles in normal everyday life (if Gerard had been correct, he would have been unable to move his own lips, let alone follow his scientific vocation), it is hardly surprising that they reject the possibility that the mind may be able to move not only the body with which it is usually associated, but something outside its own flesh and bone. But that is what psychokinesis means.

PROOF OR FRAUD?

The problem with psychokinesis for physical scientists is at least a little more straightforward. Physicists don't have to pretend to themselves that people can't think, have no feelings, and don't know a joke when they hear it; but they cannot explain how a man in a television studio in central London can cause cutlery to bend in dozens of different homes around Britain. When Uri Geller succeeded in doing just that, physicists were among the first to voice their suspicions of trickery. To a physicist, the only proper way to bend a fork is to take it in one's hands and give it a hefty twist – or subject it to rather more heat than anyone would feel comfortable having in his or her hands.

Geller's first widely noted demonstration of his extraordinary powers occurred on 23 November 1973, when he appeared as a guest on the BBC TV show *The David Dimbleby Talk-In*. Geller gently rubbed two broken watches, and both began to work again. Then he made the hands of one of these watches bend upwards – *inside the glass*, that is, without touching them. While David Dimbleby held a fork in his hand, Geller gently stroked it, and it bent. Still more astonishing, a fork lying on the studio table between Geller and Dimbleby began to bend of its own accord. The most remarkable event of the show was the producer's announcement just before it closed: that dozens of viewers had phoned in to describe how forks and spoons in their own homes had bent and twisted by themselves while the programme was on the air.

> **THE TENSION MOUNTED AS GELLER GENTLY STROKED THE FORK, WILLING IT TO BEND.**

Below: *Uri Geller at home today in Berkshire. His unusual talents are now employed largely in dowsing for mineral deposits, and bring in a handsome income from oil and mining companies.*

Astronaut Edgar Mitchell walks on the Moon (above) *during the Apollo 14 mission launched in March 1971* (right). *During this trip Mitchell attempted a number of experiments in ESP.*

Mitchell's secretary was wearing a gold ring. Geller asked her to take it off and cup it in her closed hand. Once she had done so, he then waved his hand back and forth over hers: there was no contact between them.

Feinberg reported what happened next: 'She opened her hand and the ring appeared with a crack in it, as if it had been cut through with some kind of extremely sharp instrument. Initially, there was a very small space...only a fraction of an inch. Over a few hours, the ring twisted and went gradually into the shape of an S.'

IMPOSSIBLE 'COINCIDENCES'

Geller became more ambitious as time went by. In Munich in 1972 he also appeared to have caused the Hochfelln cable car to grind to a halt in mid-air – on the fifth attempt – in answer to a journalist's challenge. The main power

Geller's mastery of metal is not his only psychic ability – he has performed extremely well in standard clairvoyance and telepathy experiments, and today enjoys a very high income from his skill at dowsing, which he uses to detect mineral deposits on behalf of international mining and oil companies. But his ability to affect a solid and intransigent material like metal is the most dramatic and demonstrable of his powers. Sceptics like the magician James Randi furiously showed how *some* of Geller's effects could be produced without calling on any paranormal abilities, but left much unexplained. And proof that fraud is possible is not, of course, proof that fraud has occurred.

A good instance of an entirely inexplicable Geller effect on metal occurred in August 1972, during his first visit to the USA. Geller was having lunch with the astronaut Edgar D. Mitchell – who, during the Apollo 14 moon mission, had carried out a number of ESP experiments from space – along with psychical researcher Dr Andrija Puharich, Gerald Feinberg (a physicist from Columbia University, New York), and Mitchell's secretary.

Far left: Cable car in mid-journey, like the one halted by Geller in 1972.

Left: Big Ben, which Geller claims to have stopped dead at 12.35 pm on 17 December 1989. The clock is famous for its accuracy and is scrupulously maintained in perfect working order – so a 'coincidence' seems an unlikely explanation for the unusual event.

switch at the control centre had apparently flipped off without warning. Given the short notice at which Geller managed this feat, it seems highly unlikely that he would have had time to organize a bribe in the right place. He was either extremely lucky, if a fraud, or he simply did what he said, and stopped the machinery by psycho-kinesis.

A few years later Geller was travelling between Spain and Italy on the liner *Renaissance*, when musicians from the ship's resident band dared him to stop the ship. Geller took up the challenge, and began to concentrate. Before long, the liner began to lose power, and finally her engines died. The ship's engineers found that the immediate cause was a crimped fuel line. Once again, the sceptical proposal that this was (for Geller) a 'lucky coincidence' is simply too feeble to contemplate. Ships' fuel lines are built to last – from metal. They don't suddenly get kinks in them of their own accord. Someone has to *put* a crimp in them, either by deliberately applied physical force – which means Geller had to have a very knowledgeable accomplice, and again in view of the short notice and spontaneous challenge, this seems a far-fetched explanation – or by some other means. Geller would appear to have used some 'other' means.

Geller's most spectacular large-scale feat took place in London in December 1989. He had been asked by an American games company to stop what is probably the world's most famous clock – *Big Ben,*

part of the British Houses of Parliament in Westminster – at midnight on New Year's Eve, 1989–90. (He has documentary proof of this request.) Geller, who was by then resident in England, went to Westminster around midday on 17 December – a day after he confirmed the deal with the company – to 'experiment'. At 12.35 pm, Big Ben stopped dead – an event almost unheard-of in the clock's history. If that was another mere 'coincidence' it was certainly a remarkable one indeed. The chances of a collaborator managing to penetrate the massive security around the Houses of Parliament are about nil. That leaves only one explanation – uncomfortable as it may be.

THERE WAS ONLY ONE EXPLANATION – AN EXPLANATION THAT MANY REFUSED TO ACCEPT.

Below: Psychokinetic effects were commonplace in Victorian spiritualist seances.

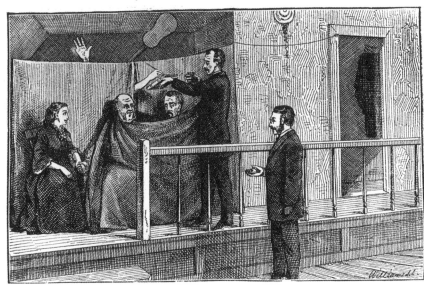

Above: *Daniel Dunglas Home's accordion – normal in every respect, except that Home was somehow able to make it play when no one was touching it.*

THE FAMILY WATCHED, MESMERIZED WITH FEAR AND AMAZEMENT, AS THE TINY HANDS MATERIALIZED OUT OF THIN AIR.

BEYOND REASONABLE DOUBT

Long before the world's television audiences were transfixed by Uri Geller, psychokinesis had been recorded and seriously researched by numerous eminent men of their day. Many psychokinetic effects were produced by spiritualist mediums in the seance rooms during the 19th century. Most of these mediums ascribed what happened while they were in trance to the activities of spirits beyond their control. A few, including one of the most remarkable of all psychics, Daniel Dunglas Home, were frankly baffled at their own abilities and did not pretend to know what was responsible for them. But as the 20th century wore on, fewer and fewer psychokinetic phenomena appeared at spiritualist seances. The present century has nevertheless been rich in people who have demonstrated these powers and have been extensively tested under controlled conditions that show beyond reasonable doubt that their powers are genuine. Few in recent years have attempted to explain the phenomena they produced as the work of spirits, but among those who did were the astonishing Schneider brothers.

Rudi and Willi Schneider were born in 1903 and 1908 respectively, in the town of Braunau, Austria (also, incidentally, the birthplace of Adolf Hitler). In 1919 the two boys began experimenting with a *planchette*. This device is said to have been invented by a German milkmaid in the 1850s, and is a handy aid to producing automatic writing. It consists of a small, thin, heart-shaped platform. Two legs or castors project from underneath it, together with a pencil. The would-be medium places the planchette on a sheet of blank paper, puts his or her fingertips on the platform, and invites the spirits to communicate.

When the Schneider boys tried it, the planchette almost immediately showed they had made contact with a spirit who called herself Olga. She said that in return for having masses said for the repose of her soul, she would make the Schneider boys world famous. The Schneider family arranged for the masses and Olga kept her promise. Willi and Rudi were indeed to startle the world with the psychokinetic phenomena they produced over the next couple of decades.

TINY HANDS

The first of these took place soon after the masses were said. Olga told the family to cover a kitchen stool with a cloth, and to put various things – among them a handkerchief and a bowl full of water – nearby. When Willi sat next to the stool, water slopped out of the bowl, some of the objects began to move, the handkerchief rose up, disappeared under the cloth on the stool and then flew out with knots tied in all four corners. Weirder yet, two tiny hands materialized from nowhere and were heard to clap.

Several things suggest that these were genuinely paranormal events. First, they happened simultaneously – so that any ordinary degree of sleight of hand can be ruled out. Second, Willi, at 16 years of age, seems a trifle young to have developed such extraordinary powers of prestidigitation, even if the number and complexity of the phenomena did not make this too facile an explanation. And there is the testimony of one of the independent witnesses, a Captain Kogelnik, to consider:

'Not even the slightest attempt was made by [Willi] to support the supernormal phenomena through normal means. He never fell into trance; he himself watched the manifestations with as much interest as any other person present.'

Willi's abilities soon attracted the

attention of a number of scientists and other interested parties. By May 1922, 30 professors, 20 doctors, and 16 other 'savants' (one of them a general of the army, one the renowned novelist Thomas Mann) had witnessed or investigated Willi. After one seance in which a bell, which had been standing in Mann's full view on the floor, began to ring loudly of its own accord, he noted: 'Any thought of a swindle in the sense of a conjuring trick is absurd. There was simply nobody there who could have rung the bell.' Mann had arrived in sceptical mood.

Dr Eric Dingwall of the British Society for Psychical Research spent considerable effort in looking for hidden trapdoors, false walls and systems of pulleys in the Schneider household in Braunau's Stadtplatz, but found no sign that any conventional mechanism or trickery could account for the effects. Despite producing some remarkable phenomena, Willi's powers began to fade after 1922, but by then his brother Rudi had begun exhibiting his own paranormal talents.

Rudi Schneider's capacity for psychokinesis was thoroughly tested by the French psychical researcher Eugene Osty in Paris in 1931, and with fascinating results. Osty had realized that the key to proving the genuineness of any psychokinetic event lay in showing that nothing material had touched any of the objects that moved. Osty and his son Marcel, who was an engineer, devised a detection system that surrounded the 'target' objects with infra-red light. Anything – such as a human hand intent on a hoax – that broke the infra-red beams would automatically trigger a flash camera.

What actually happened was not what anyone expected. Rudi went into trance with various objects at a distance from where he was sitting. Olga 'came through' and announced she would pick up a handkerchief. The moment the handkerchief moved, however, the flashbulb exploded into life. Expecting to find evidence of trickery, Osty was mystified when the resulting photograph showed the handkerchief moving but no sign that anything material was interfering with it. He could only explain the result by inferring that his apparatus was faulty.

But the same thing happened several times more, even after Osty had made absolutely sure that his equipment was working perfectly. He eventually concluded that something paranormal was interfering with the infra-red beams. In due course, Olga – or whatever psycho-physical aspect of Rudi Schneider 'she' personified – interfered directly with the infra-red rays to trigger the camera on demand. Osty also found that the rays were affected

Top: *Thomas Mann, one of many distinguished witnesses to Willi Schneider's remarkable powers of psychokinesis. Initially sceptical, Mann was completely convinced of the genuineness of Schneider's abilities when he saw them demonstrated.*

Left: *Rudi Schneider is tested by psychical researcher Baron von Schrenck-Notzing in 1922.*

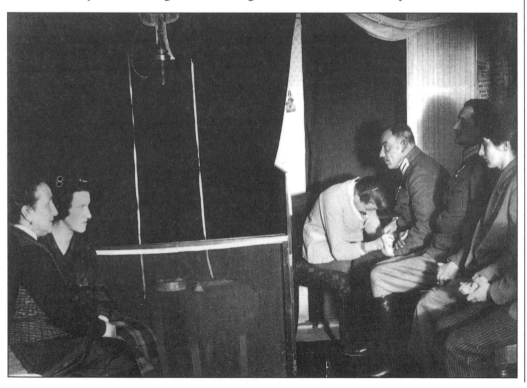

differently when Olga broke them than when they were broken by a material object. These experiments have been hailed by historians of psychical research as perhaps the most important of all investigations into psychokinesis.

EYELESS SIGHT

Just a few years before Uri Geller made headlines, Western parapsychologists had become intrigued by remarkable film featuring a former Red Army tank radio operator. The Russian ex-sergeant was a lady from Leningrad, born in 1928, called Nelya, or 'Nina', Kulagina.

Kulagina had first interested medical

THE RED ARMY TANK RADIO OPERATOR FOUND THAT SHE COULD SEE THINGS WITHOUT USING HER EYES.

the results began to appear in the West, and it was these that aroused the interest of researchers there.

Kulagina's psychokinetic abilities never reached the grandiose heights of Uri Geller's later effect on Big Ben, but they were extremely varied in effect – and certainly no less intriguing.

GROTESQUE EXPERIMENTS

The Leningrad researchers reported that Kulagina psychokinetically moved small aluminium pipes and a box of matches over a distance of 3 in. In one of the films, she is seen to make a ping-pong ball levitate and hover in the air. In another, various small objects could be seen moving around under her influence inside a sealed transparent jar. For some strange reason, long or cylindrical objects – such as cigarettes or pencils – would stand on end before moving across the laboratory table.

In 1970, a team of American researchers went to Leningrad to watch Kulagina at work for themselves. They noted the variety of different materials that she could affect, from metals and plastics to paper and fabrics; and that objects moved quite inconsistently, sometimes in fits and starts and sometimes slowly and steadily, although never very far. In one test Kulagina made a solid gold wedding ring

Above: *Joe Mangini, a member of the SORRAT psychic research group based in Rolla, Missouri, bends a spoon – although it is sealed inside the bottle in his hand – on 3 January 1978.*

Right: *Monica Nieto Tejada with a strip of metal that she bent using psychokinesis.*

scientists at Leningrad's Institute of Brain Research in the 1960s, when she had discovered that she could detect the colours of sewing threads simply by touching them. In early experiments she also found that she could read newsprint by running her finger across the printed paper.

While these tests were being done, the researchers noticed that whenever Kulagina was practising her 'eyeless sight', any small object near her fingertips would move away from her. The discovery inspired a new, and quite different, series of tests. Film as well as published reports of

turn in circles as she rotated her head above it. The possibility that she was using a magnet hidden in her mouth to create the effect is ruled out by the fact that gold does not respond to ordinary iron magnets and, the Americans observed, rigorous precautions were taken to ensure that Kulagina could not conceal such useful aids to fraud about her person.

Possibly the most extraordinary facet of Kulagina's power was her ability to affect living flesh. In one somewhat grotesque experiment a frog's heart was removed alive from its body. Normally, in these circumstances, the extracted organ will carry on beating at its usual rate for as long as four hours. Kulagina concentrated on this one, and slowed its pulse rate until it stopped beating altogether after only 12 minutes. In other experiments she simply laid her hand on another person's arm – with the result that they felt an extraordinary burning heat, which could be genuinely painful. Some subjects actually suffered burn marks on their skin.

BAFFLING SCIENCE

These are the most famous of those who have shown psychokinetic powers, but they are not alone. In the 1970s, too, the Muscovite Alla Vinogravada showed that she could make objects weighing up to 3 oz roll across a tabletop, and make those weighing a third of that slide across the surface they were resting on – all without touching them. New Yorker Felicia Parise demonstrated similar powers in tests at the Maimonides Medical Center in New York City, although it was only with great effort

and emotional tension that she succeeded, and then only with very small objects. In 1978, Joe Mangini of Columbia, Missouri, used psychokinesis to bend cutlery that had been sealed out of reach inside a bottle. In similar tests in 1989, the 15-year-old Spanish girl Monica Nieto Tejada bent metal strips sealed into glass tubes by holding them to her forehead and concentrating hard.

Earlier in the 1980s, several English schoolchildren convincingly demonstrated psychokinetic abilities in tests run by Professor John Hasted of the University of London. In a spin-off from this series of experiments, one schoolboy, Mark Briscoe, performed a truly remarkable feat in 1982, using wire made from the 'memory metal' nitinol. This alloy wire has the curious property of permanently holding its shape – that is, if it is bent out of its pre-formed shape, it will simply revert to its original configuration. The only way to reshape it permanently is – ostensibly – through heat-treatment under tension at temperatures of around 900° F. Mark Briscoe managed to produce a permanent alteration in *his* length of nitinol wire simply by stroking it.

As a change – some experimenters doubtless found it a welcome relief from watching cutlery bend – in 1984, the Polish teenager Joasia Gajewski managed to put a fork into free flight across a room in front of Japanese TV cameras. This was itself a change from her usual routine, which was to make lightbulbs explode at will.

No wonder the scientists are embarrassed as well as baffled.

Left: *Professor John B. Hasted of the University of London, who has conducted thousands of experiments that have satisfied him of the reality of psychokinesis. Hasted, in company with other distinguished physicists, suspects that quantum mechanics may hold clues to the mystery of how mind can affect matter so powerfully.*

KULAGINA CONCENTRATED ON THE PULSATING HEART, DETERMINED TO STOP IT BEATING FOR EVER.

Below: *These paperclips, held inside a glass sphere, safely away from physical interference by any means except the application of powerful magnets, were tangled together by the psychic power of a schoolchild.*

THE SORRAT STORY

Some considered Neihardt a charlatan and a fraud; others reserved judgement, but only the Oglala Sioux knew the truth about his astonishing powers. He founded the controversial society that set out to prove that pens write by themselves and metal rings could interlink without a single break.

In a basement in Rolla, Missouri, a pen sits up by itself and at lightning speed scribbles a message on a piece of paper. Two seamless leather rings shuffle toward each other. Without a break appearing in either of them, one ring connects with the other, and they interlink. Then they flip apart. Still, neither is broken. A letter, addressed to a person in another country, is left in a sealed container without stamps on it. It disappears – and turns up a few days later at the correct address bearing a US postmark but Equadorian, not US Mail, stamps …

And so it goes on. The catalogue of major psychokinetic events that have taken place as a result of the work of the Society for Research into Rapport and Telekinesis (SORRAT), based in Rolla, is now

enormous. The group has been working together since 1961, and was established with the deliberate intention of bringing forth, once again, some of the more spectacular psychokinetic manifestations that amazed and graced the seance rooms of the Victorian era. Needless to say, SORRAT has met with its share and more of controversy in the years since 1961.

The arch-sceptic James Randi has said that he cannot believe anyone would take SORRAT's work seriously, and that it is 'not any more worth refuting than the Santa Claus myth'. Others have reserved judgement on the group's claims, but acknowledge that it has established a

Opposite: *Dr John G. Neihardt, poet, honorary member of the Sioux nation, and founder of SORRAT, at the age of 90 in 1972. With him is his secretary, Florence Boring.*

Above: *SORRAT researcher and experimental director W.E. Cox searches for the exact location of paranormal raps heard coming from the ground during a group session in September 1976.*

Left: *Skyrim Farm at Columbia, Missouri, where the SORRAT group first met under the guidance of Dr Neihardt in the hope of reproducing the kind of physical phenomena common in Victorian seance rooms.*

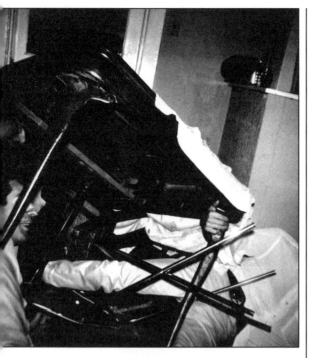

Left: *Two SORRAT members tangle with an 80 lb table as it crashes to the floor after levitating to ceiling height during a session in July 1966.*

Right: *A small table rises into the air at a SORRAT meeting with no physical assistance.*

method of investigating psychokinesis that should be a model for all researchers. Others acclaim the films and stills of the phenomena as a brilliant record, a more than reasonable proof, of the reality of psychokinesis. Meanwhile, SORRAT, unmoved, continue their work, and stand by their story.

What is that story?

PARANORMAL RAPPINGS

SORRAT was founded by Dr John G. Neihardt who, apart from being professor of English literature at the University of Missouri at Columbia, Mo., and poet

> **WHAT WAS MORE SIGNIFICANT WAS WHAT NEIHARDT CHOSE NOT TO REVEAL IN HIS BOOK.**

Below: *The apparition of 'Myra', which appeared to SORRAT members at Skyrim Farm on 27 June 1967. Myra had first communicated to the group using raps, telling them she had been a student at the University of Missouri and had died in about 1869.*

laureate of his native state of Nebraska, was the author of *Black Elk Speaks*. This extraordinary narrative, written in the 1930s, was the product of Neihardt's long and close friendship with the Oglala Sioux shaman Black Elk, and has been recognized as of enormous anthropological importance. The Oglala Sioux appreciated Neihardt enough to honour him with honorary membership of their tribe. Of more importance to psychical research, however, may be what Neihardt did not put in that book.

There is some evidence that Neihardt was himself initiated as a shaman, which implies that he had unusual mental, emotional and psychic strength – and physical stamina as well. Part of the shaman's task as a spiritual hub of the tribe is to make direct contact with the spirit world, which may be done through using hallucinogenic or psychotropic drugs; through drumming, dance and song, or ascetic, yoga-like exercises of self-deprivation; and often all of these together.

Whether the climactic shamanic 'flight' into the Otherworld to bring its wisdom back to the world of mortals is a real spiritual journey, an out-of-the-body experience, or an elaborate mystical illusion, no one who has not undertaken it can even begin to guess. But, whether or not Neihardt himself made this journey, his friend Black Elk certainly had; and the poet from Nebraska developed both a stern respect for the world of the spirit and a fascination for the paranormal. What particularly intrigued Neihardt was the fact that people with a powerful belief in a world of spirit could generate – or perhaps

it was attract – psychokinetic effects. SORRAT was founded in part to explore that relationship.

In its early years SORRAT met every Friday evening at Neihardt's home at Skyrim Farm near Columbia. There was no solemn ritual involved; the group – the hard core numbered between 15 and 20 – simply sat about talking and joking and waiting for something to happen. Everyone recognized that months might pass before anything occurred; but the notion of 'rapport' among the members of the group, without which nothing would happen, was central to the SORRAT philosophy.

The first noticeable phenomenon was a peculiar coldness that surrounded objects left on a table during the sessions. Measurements showed them to be as much as 5° F colder than the surrounding room temperature. Within a few months, paranormal rappings began.

The raps were, it soon transpired, undoubtedly disembodied. They moved around the room on request, when everyone's hands and feet were visible, and even continued to sound outside the house, when they seemed to come from under the ground. Next, the group set up a code to communicate with the 'agency' – their carefully chosen neutral term for whatever was causing the sounds. Using the code they gradually encouraged the 'agency' to graduate to carry out simple 'tasks' – and to complete them would require some manifestation of psychokinesis.

By 1966 the SORRAT group had managed to levitate a massive oak table weighing 82 lb, and keep a light metal tray in the air – with no one touching it – for a full three minutes. Other effects were beginning to emerge, as well: mysterious lights appeared, objects appeared in the midst of the group as if from nowhere, others moved paranormally from place to place. Once, a life-like apparition materialized on the lawn outside Skyrim Farm, and was photographed. The 'agency' maintained that this was 'Myra', who had died over a century before.

FRAUD DETECTIVE

In 1969 there was a new development. Dr J.B. Rhine, professor of psychology and director of the Parapsychology Laboratory at Duke University, Durham, North Carolina, had long been interested in Neihardt's work with SORRAT, and now suggested that the phenomena were so persistent and on such a scale that some professional help might be useful in gathering proof that they were indeed occurring. He offered the services of William E. Cox, his chief field investigator into psychokinesis. Cox had some 20 years' experience in researching psychokinesis, and was also a trained magician. Not only was he therefore well qualified to detect fraud, he also, as a result, knew how to prevent it.

One obvious solution to the problem of fraud – or even accusations of fraud – was

a locked container in which the 'agency' could be invited to do its work. Neihardt built a huge transparent chamber for the purpose, but the results were poor. Cox decided to take a leaf out of the original SORRAT book, and work gradually towards a fully sealed and equipped container. He decided to start with shallow wooden boxes, with transparent lids and simple seals, in which relatively minor psychokinetic effects could occur and be photographed.

These became known in the annals of SORRAT as 'coffee boxes', because more often than not the bottom of these sealed

SLOWLY, UNBELIEVABLY, THE MASSIVE OAK TABLE ROSE IN THE AIR TOWARDS THE CEILING.

Above: A 'coffee box', showing trails in the coffee grounds left by objects that were paranormally moved across the box's base.

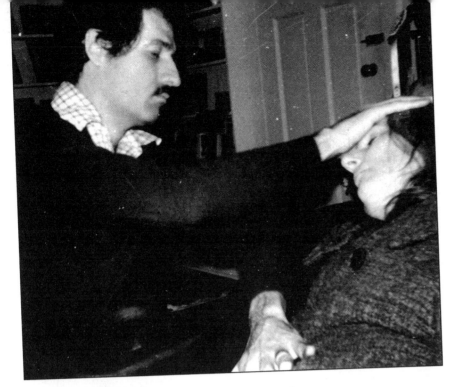

Above: *SORRAT member Joe Mangini performs psychic healing on Mrs Elaine Richards.*

trays was lightly and evenly covered in coffee grounds to track any movement of the objects inside. The coffee grounds also helped prevent the movement being effected by tilting the box, since they would reveal what had happened – by simply heaping up at one side or one end. A typical experiment was to put two dice in the box and ask the 'agency' to move only one – which it did successfully, and left tracks in the coffee grounds. Again, tilting the box would have made both dice move, and obscured any tracks.

Other boxes held nothing but carbon paper and a stylus. The 'agency' was invited to leave written messages by pressing the stylus on the carbon paper, so marking the pale wooden floor of the box. The results varied from meaningless scrawls to whole words. These early 'direct writing' experiments, though successful in their way, were to develop into something far more remarkable and elaborate in the years to come.

In 1973, SORRAT's founder, John G. Neihardt, died. As a result of that loss the group at Skyrim wavered somewhat in its purpose, but already a new and astonishing phenomenon was emerging with a few individuals. As a consequence, no doubt, of a dozen years' practice in letting psychokinetic events come forth, two of the founder members of SORRAT, Dr John Thomas Richards and Joseph Mangini were beginning to experience spontaneous psychokinesis in their everyday lives.

William Cox retired from the Para-psychology Laboratory at Duke in 1977, and settled in Rolla to monitor the psychokinesis that was occurring around Richards. Cox had made the extraordinary discovery that psychokinesis was possible even without the encouragement of the group when checking the state of the 'coffee boxes' at Skyrim, and – most astonishing of all – that psychokinesis would occur even when no one was even thinking about the boxes, SORRAT, or the group, let alone psychokinesis as such.

SEALED AND PADLOCKED

It was now time to put the achievements of SORRAT on record, and in a way that would, as far as possible, show that the psychokinetic effects they were able to produce were genuine.

(For those already convinced of the reality of psychic phenomena, SORRAT's greatest creation, out of infinite patience and dedication, was the circumstances in which spontaneous psychokinesis could occur at all. For psychical researchers, the invention of the mini-lab that followed as a direct consequence was an equally important accomplishment, if not more so. Here was a tool that could be deployed and adapted in a seemingly endless variety of ways not simply to test for psychokinesis, but to prove that it had occurred.)

The means Cox hit upon for this purpose was the 'mini-lab' – an elaboration on the original transparent chamber constructed by Neihardt. The first was a lidless Perspex™ box that was inverted to stand with its open side sealed against a heavy wooden base by steel strips and two heavy-duty padlocks. Inside it, Cox placed a number of objects, which the 'agency' was asked to manipulate in various ways. This spent some time at Skyrim before being moved to Dr Richards's home in Rolla, near Columbia.

Interesting things happened there. On one occasion Cox had set the mini-lab up in Dr Richards's sitting room. Inside the container were (among other things) a pencil and paper, dried peas that had been dyed white and blue, a small glass tumbler, some leather rings, pipecleaners, and six cotton spools strung on a wire that was twisted at the ends to hold them together. Dr Richards and a number of friends

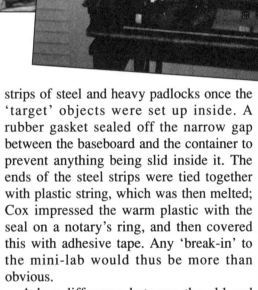

simply sat down in the room, turned out the light, and waited. In due course, noises came from the sealed mini-lab, and eventually stopped. When the light was turned on again, things inside the container were not quite as they had been – although the seals were unbroken and the locks still secure.

One of the six cotton spools had apparently vanished. The wire on which it had been strung had been retwisted. The glass tumbler now held 30 blue dried peas. The leather rings had moved. Two pipe-cleaners had been twisted into rings that were linked together.

The obvious difficulty about this event as evidence was that the only testimony to its truth was from those who had taken part in the session – and from Cox, who had arrived toward the end of the apparent movements inside the mini-lab. It was obvious that some kind of independent recording of what went on in the mini-lab, as it was happening, was necessary. Cox found a collaborator in a Mr S. Calvin, who helped to design and build a mini-lab that would provide the kind of evidence Cox wanted.

ASTOUNDING EVENTS

The new mini-labs were once again made of a transparent tank, upturned and capable of being sealed against a hefty base with strips of steel and heavy padlocks once the 'target' objects were set up inside. A rubber gasket sealed off the narrow gap between the baseboard and the container to prevent anything being slid inside it. The ends of the steel strips were tied together with plastic string, which was then melted; Cox impressed the warm plastic with the seal on a notary's ring, and then covered this with adhesive tape. Any 'break-in' to the mini-lab would thus be more than obvious.

A key difference between the old and new mini-labs lay in how the objects inside were set up. They were now placed on, or linked to, highly sensitive microswitches that would operate immediately if anything attached to them moved. These switches triggered lights and an 8 mm movie camera, which was linked to a timing device so that it would take 30 seconds of film every time a switch flipped on. A digital clock stood in front of the mini-lab to record when the events took place.

Two of these carefully prepared devices were put in the basement of Dr Richards's home in Rolla during the spring of 1979. It was here that the most remarkable of the SORRAT evidence for psychokinesis has been filmed, with reactions ranging from

Above left: *W.E. Cox demonstrates the locked and sealed 'mini-lab' used at Rolla. The container is designed to prevent any physical interference with the objects inside. If these move under psychokinetic influence, a movie camera is triggered to film the paranormal events as they happen.*

Above: *A similarly set up mini-lab in the laboratory of Dr Berthold Schwarz, in Vero Beach, Florida.*

THE SEALS WERE UNBROKEN AND THE PADLOCKS STILL SECURE – BUT INSIDE THE CONTAINER, IT WAS ANOTHER MATTER.

Above: *Paper rings link and catch fire during an experiment at Rolla in early 1992.*

Far right: *One of the most astonishing of the effects seen at Rolla. Inside the mini-lab, a pen writes a message without the assistance of a human hand.*

Right: *A message from the 'agencies' at work within the mini-lab, insisting that they are surviving spirits of the dead.*

dismissiveness or rage on the part of sceptics, to undisguised and unadulterated delight on the part of believers.

The list of astounding events that have occurred since then in the mini-labs would fill many pages. But even a brief summary could not exclude the following:

• *Spontaneous combustions*
Film exists showing a candle igniting of its own accord inside the sealed mini-lab. As a result the glass container cracked. Film also shows paper bursting into flames by itself – either effect would be difficult to achieve as a 'special effect', or in cruder terms, as a deliberate hoax.

• *Metal bending*
Spoons, forks and plain strips of metal left inside the mini-lab have been distorted by psychokinesis and the process has been recorded on film.

• *Spontaneous inflations*
Balloons have often inflated themselves inside the mini-lab. One such occasion was independently filmed by the production crew of the Yorkshire Television series *Arthur C. Clarke's World of Mysterious Powers* on Labor Day 1983.

• *Direct writing*
There are many instances on record of pens taking it upon themselves to write messages without the intervention of any human agency, and at extraordinary speed. William E. Cox estimates that direct writing occurs at twice the average human writing speed at least. The quality of the messages received varies from the banal through the metaphysical to the unashamedly jokey in rhyming verse.

Left: The block of marble (immediately to the left of the cylindrical container) placed by Dr Berthold Schwarz in the Rolla mini-lab with a request for the initials of a dead friend to be written on it. The picture was taken before the marble was placed in the mini-lab.

HIS DEAD FRIEND'S INITIALS WERE CARVED DEEPLY INTO THE COLD MARBLE.

Below: The marble after its sojourn in the mini-lab, clearly showing the letters CM – the initials of Dr Schwarz's dead friend – inscribed on it. No one was near the mini-lab when the inscription occurred, and none of those present knew what initials Dr Schwarz was hoping to see appear on the marble.

On Easter Sunday 1991 an exceptional result was had from an experiment proposed by Dr Berthold Schwarz and set up in a plastic box with a cardboard liner at Skyrim Farm. In the container were a pencil stub and a block of marble, plus a note from Dr Schwarz requesting the 'agency' to give the initials of the person to whom the marble block was important. The box was left in the Skyrim study while a group of SORRAT members waited in the living room. Nothing happened for over an hour, and the group was ready to decide that nothing would, when the phone rang.

On the line was Maria Hanna, a SORRAT member living in Barstow, California; she had just had a series of paranormal raps in her home that, using the usual code, had said that a poem had appeared at Skyrim. Ms Hanna had had no idea that a SORRAT meeting was in session until she called. The group headed as one for the study to check the box. Inside, written in pencil on the cardboard liner, were the following lines:

I am you and you are I!
When the world is cherished most,
You shall hear my haunting cry,
See me rising like a ghost.
I am all that you have been,
Are not now, but soon shall be!
Thralled a while by dust and din –
Brother, Brother, follow me!

This, says Dr Richards, is a stanza from Dr Neihardt's poem 'The Ghostly Brother'. Yet more astonishing was what had happened to Berthold Schwarz's block of marble. Carved into it were the letters 'CM'. When told of this, Dr Schwarz confirmed that these were the initials he

had been hoping to have communicated (and that he had been keeping to himself). He then revealed that the marble came from the face of a building that had been named in memory of 'C.M.', who had been a close friend of Dr Schwarz and was now dead.

• *Linking rings*

It has long been a goal of para-psychological researchers to prove the successful working of psychokinesis by achieving the permanent interlinking of two separate rings of some seamless material – wood, leather, or metal, for instance. SORRAT films show momentary interlinking of leather rings (each cut from a single piece of hide). Messages from Cox and Richards to the 'agency' had persistently requested this achievement, but to no avail. One directly written response said testily: 'We've tried, but can't make the damn leather rings stay linked – sorry.' Another time, the 'agency' answered: 'When the psi energy is sufficient, we shall try to do this for you. However, do not expect to overcome the envious prejudice of your inferiors...'

However, in 1985, a metallurgist known only as Donald C. created two rings of a unique metal alloy whose formula only he knew. During an experiment at Skyrim Farm, the rings linked – and stayed that way. According to Dr Richards, 'Careful laboratory analysis shows that there is no cut or break in the metal of either ring.'

• *Levitations and extractions*

Film has shown the leather rings that are usually installed in the mini-lab, as well as numerous other objects, rising into the air of their own accord. Film has also shown letters being extracted from – and through – the envelopes that contain them, although the envelopes (and, of course, the mini-lab) have clearly remained sealed as the paper has come forth.

• *Psychokinetic sortings*

The original mini-lab event has been repeated more than once, with dyed dried

Above and right: *Rings placed inside the mini-lab before an experiment in December 1985 are clearly separate, but on retrieval after the experiment are no less clearly linked, without being broken or marked in any way.*

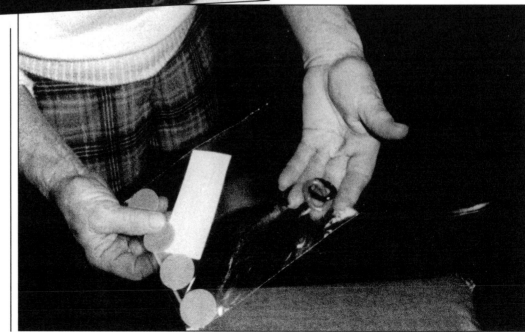

peas that have been left in the mini-lab in a mixed assortment of colours sorting themselves into single-colour groups.

• *Card calling*
Sealed sets of Zener cards, fresh from the makers and packed in random order, have been left in the mini-lab, and the 'agency' has been asked to call the order of the cards. Responses have been acquired through paranormal rapping, direct writing, and other means, and in about one attempt in three have been absolutely accurate for the whole run of the pack. In one unusual experiment conducted in 1991, Cox placed a blank audio tape next to a sealed pack of ordinary playing cards, which are always sold shuffled in random order. When the audio tape was taken from the mini-lab it was found to have on it a recording of a 'soft, feminine voice with an Arabic accent', correctly calling the order of the entire 52 cards in the deck – which remained sealed.

• *Apports*
Film exists of a piece of typewriting appearing from nowhere in front of the mini-lab. Other, mundane objects have also appeared inside the mini-lab.

• *Teleports*
Possibly the most controversial of all SORRAT's claims is that objects have been placed inside the sealed mini-lab and then appeared elsewhere with no human intervention. The first time this occurred was in May 1979, when Cox secured a green felt-tipped pen inside the container – and later found it on the floor of Dr Richards's basement, although the mini-lab remained untouched. Materials as varied as pipecleaners, water, matchbooks, peas, mica sheets, string, jewellery, film, and paper have transported themselves in or out of mini-labs. Films show such items appearing and disappearing and, yet more astonishing, actually passing through the glass of the sealed container.

These events led the experimenters to leave sealed, addressed, but unstamped letters inside the mini-lab to discover whether or not they would find their way to their intended destinations. They did. Often the letters have been adorned with unusual postage stamps – South American, Italian and even Australian ones have been attached to the envelopes – although they have all reached their destinations by way of the US Mail Office in Rolla and bear the Rolla postmark.

Above: *Another set of rings, put separately into the Rolla mini-lab, link spontaneously and without a break in the material.*

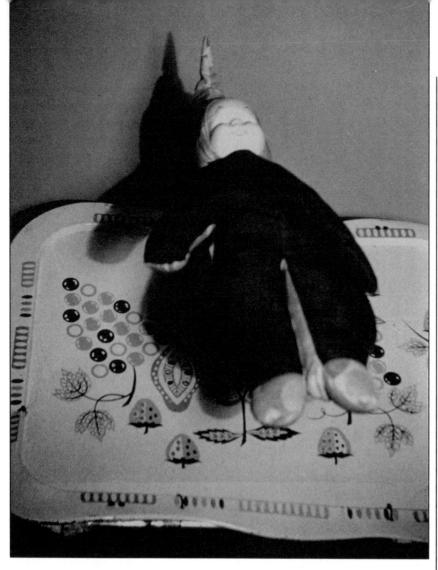

Above: *A doll levitates from a tray during a SORRAT session.*

THE LIGHTBULB WAS STILL UNBROKEN AND FIXED TO ITS BASE CONNECTOR, BUT THE COCKROACH WAS NOW TRAPPED INSIDE IT.

A number of psychical researchers around the world have received such letters, and during the Yorkshire TV filming mentioned previously, the production team left one – sealed but unstamped – in the mini-lab for paranormal posting to Arthur C. Clarke, along with several quarters (25-cent pieces), which were not in the envelope. Two weeks later, the letter and one of the quarters disappeared from the mini-lab. Both – with the missing quarter now in the envelope, which had somehow acquired stamps to the correct value for airmail – turned up at Clarke's residence in Sri Lanka shortly afterward.

One of the more startling teleports that the mini-lab achieved involved a living creature. In January 1992, psychiatrist and parapsychologist Dr Berthold E. Schwarz provided SORRAT with a large Florida cockroach from his home state and an ordinary clear lightbulb, with the request to the 'agency' behind the mini-lab to put the roach into the lightbulb. According to Dr Richards's testimony, 'the cockroach, some

white packing powder, and two slips of paper with notes paranormally written on them entered the sealed bulb'. One of the notes was written paranormally by the 'agency' to a SORRAT member, Eilly Fithian. The lightbulb remained unbroken and sealed to its base connector.

• *Paranormal sounds*
In another experiment using audio tape, Cox pre-recorded a cassette from beginning to end with the sound of a clock ticking. He left this tape in the mini-lab, again without a recorder. When it was retrieved and played, the tape also now held the sound of a series of paranormal raps – but the sound of the ticking clock had not been erased.

CONTROLLING SPIRIT

Who, or what, is responsible for the psychokinesis in the mini-labs and other SORRAT experiments? What is the 'agency'?

Opinions differ on this among SORRAT members themselves. Some believe the 'agency' is a product of members of the group's own subconscious. Some, including Dr Richards, prefer to think of the 'agency' as a group of spirits. The 'agency' itself has not always been consistent on this point. It has referred to itself by name, but at least once insisted that this particular personality resided in 'the fifth level of the subconscious' of one of the SORRAT members.

In the very first rapping experiments at Skyrim in the 1960s, the group asked whatever was behind the raps to identify itself. The answer was 'John King', the name of a spirit control (and long-dead pirate) that has allegedly acted as an intermediary between this world and the next for several mediums, including two of the most famous – and notorious – of the 19th century, Eusapia Palladino and Florence Cook. Since King announced 'himself' to SORRAT, a number of other names of alleged spirits or entities have cropped up in direct writing or through other communications. They have names like Explicator, Rector, Imperator, Mentor, IIIxIII, Eowald, and Expeditor – as well as, more mundanely, Sam, Mickey and Grady. Taken together these sound like the cast of some old-time spaceflight-and-sorcery

radio serial. Whether they are genuinely disembodied entities (as they themselves claim) who happen to like slightly camp science fiction, or useful dramatizations from the collective unconscious of the SORRAT group, has to remain an open question.

Most psychical researchers would agree that the true answer to that question doesn't matter, for the time being at least. The value of the SORRAT work does not lie in any evidence it might contain for survival after physical death. The value of the independence of the alleged entities is that their manifestation removed any responsibility for producing paranormal effects from the members of the group. Apart from increasing the general relaxation of the meetings, so facilitating the 'rapport' that Neihardt believed to be crucial to producing psychokinesis, this lack of individual responsibility also meant that no particular member of the group would be deemed indispensable to the production of psychical phenomena. And it is the variety, depth and range of the psychokinetic effects that SORRAT has produced that is so impressive.

HOAX EXPOSED?

SORRAT's other great achievement is the invention of the mini-lab. It can, of course, be improved. Two cameras at right angles to each other, with a third giving a wide-angle, panoramic view of the whole ensemble and its background would vastly reduce the set-up's vulnerability to fraud, as would either enclosing the cameras within the chamber or sealing the room in which the lab is placed with as much attention as has been devoted to the mini-lab itself. A 24-hour digital clock showing local time to the second as well as the date would both pinpoint events in time and verify the accuracy of timing of the camera runs. Using video cameras rather than movie film would improve the quality of the 'proof', as well – if only by reducing the opportunities sceptics have of crying 'Hoax!' and producing hilarious, but pointless, stop-action home movies of their own that purport to 'expose' the SORRAT work as fraudulent.

SORRAT has produced two major breakthroughs in psychical research: spontaneous, large-scale, and persistent psychokinetic phenomena; and the basis of a research tool that no serious para-psychologist interested in psychokinesis should be without. What will they do next?

Left: *The message in this sealed bottle was written when an alleged psychic exerted conscious psychokinesis across a room during a SORRAT session. At the same time the safety-pin closed and the pipe-cleaners bent themselves into a stick figure.*

Below: *A Florida cockroach that was left inside the mini-lab with a plain lightbulb has been apported into the lightbulb – along with paper and white powder that, according to a message from the 'agencies' behind the event, was necessary 'to prevent breakage'.*

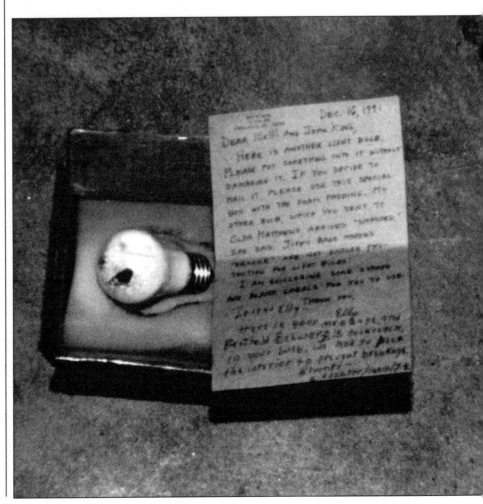

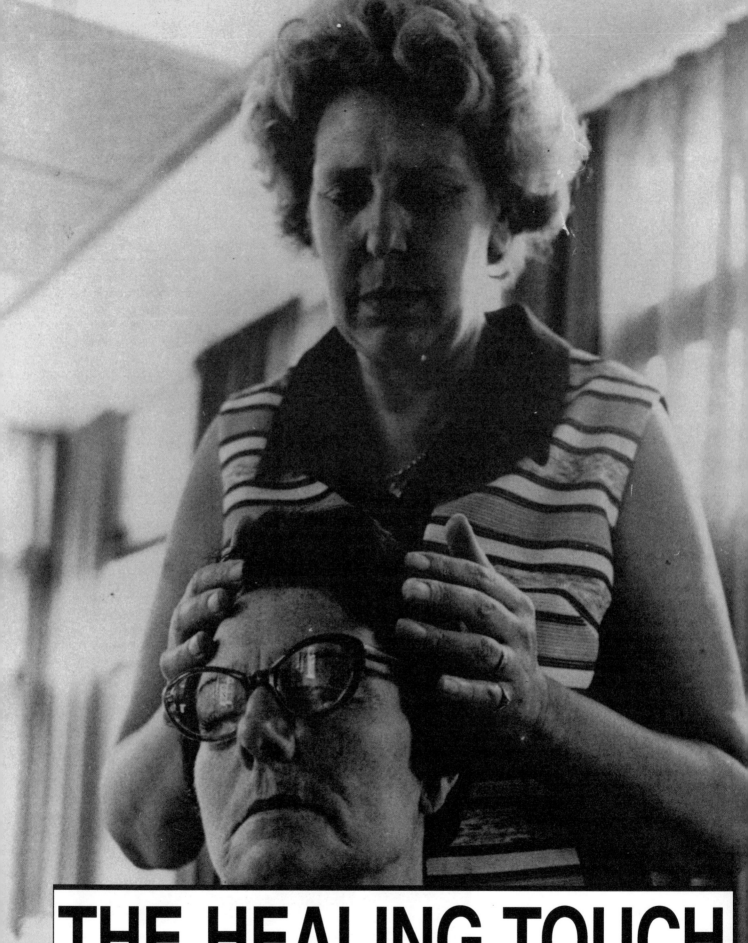

THE HEALING TOUCH

The sudden discovery that she was a healer brought Rose Gladden great joy. It was only later that she realized the gift could also be a burden that would drive her to the very edge of madness.

At the age of 19, in the 1940s, Rose Gladden discovered she was a healer.

'I had gone into a shop in London called Dyers and Chapman and found Mr Chapman, who had collapsed, lying under the counter. I asked him what was wrong and he said, "I'm in terrible pain. I have an ulcer."

'Now I didn't know where that ulcer was. All I thought was, "I wish I could help him," and I heard a voice say, "You can. Put your hand there."

'"But where?" I asked myself. "He hasn't told me where this ulcer is."

'With that I saw a little star, just as if it had fallen out of the night sky, floating over his left shoulder and, as I watched, the star floated down and stopped on the top half of the stomach.

'Mr Chapman confirmed that was where the ulcer was. As I put my hand there, I never saw but felt another hand come over mine and hold it steady. I felt my hand being filled with a tremendous heat. I couldn't move it away. It was as if it was glued to that part of the body. After a while, my hand was pulled like a magnet to his side and then away from his body.

'With that, he said, "That's gone, it's marvellous. Your fingers felt as if they were holding the pain and as you took your hand across, the pain went with it."

'I was absolutely overjoyed. I still didn't know you called it healing. I just knew I was beginning to realize why I was born and what I had to do was help people.'

THE PRICE TO BE PAID

Successful, unexpected and apparently simple as this discovery was, Rose Gladden did not find the process of

Opposite: *Healer Rose Gladden gives the healing touch.*

HER HAND WAS BURNING HOT AND, FRIGHTENED, SHE TRIED TO PULL IT AWAY.

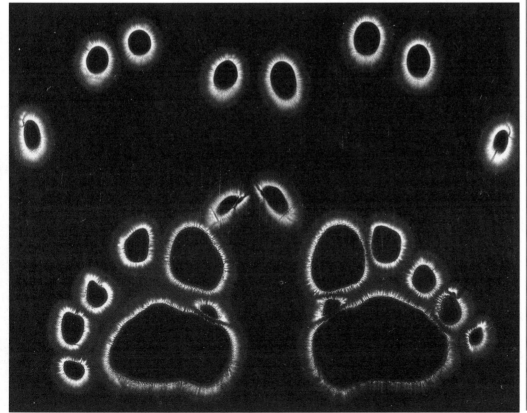

Left: *A Kirlian 'photograph' of fingertips and toes. The Kirlian technique detects static electricity on the surface of the skin – not, as some have claimed, the human aura that some psychics are apparently able to detect, or yet more fanciful attributes such as astrological or cheiromantic characteristics. Used by an experienced practitioner with proper medical training, the Kirlian technique can be an extremely useful diagnostic tool.*

becoming a full-time healer by any means easy. Since childhood she had seen 'forms and beings' that other people could not see; then, after her experience with Mr Chapman, during her twenties, she had a series of psychic experiences that were so intense and disturbing that she thought she might go mad. Today, she says she had to suffer in order to learn, and that without that distressing episode her work would be less effective. Although she is a psychic, not a 'spiritual' healer, and does not call on a spirit guide in her healing, she does believe that a spirit world exists and that it contains malignant as well as benign entities.

Rose Gladden has two ways of deciding how to go about treating a patient. She sometimes sees silver lines and spots mapped out on people's bodies, showing where the root of a particular complaint lies. She was at first mystified by the fact that these often showed in quite different places from where patients complained of suffering pain, although treating them (by laying her hands on the spot where the light showed) would effect a cure. It was years before she discovered that the lines and spots corresponded precisely with the lines and 'meridians' in the body identified by acupuncturists.

Rose Gladden is also one of those who claims to be able to see the human aura. This has been variously defined: as 'an envelope of vital energy, which apparently radiates from everything in nature' (from Harper's *Encyclopedia of Mystical and Paranormal Experience*); as 'a spiritual sphere surrounding everyone' (Swedenborg); as the physical body's 'etheric double' (Dr Walter J. Kilner, *The Human Aura*); some writers also identify the aura as the 'astral body' that is capable of leaving and returning to the physical body. A curiosity of the aura is that no two psychics see it in the same way, and often differ in their interpretations of the various bands of colour they are able to see in it, but there is general agreement that any physical sickness is reflected as disturbances in the aura, and may show there long before pain or other symptoms appear in the body.

Rose Gladden interprets this in an interesting way. She maintains that physical maladies are the *result* of imbalances and blockages of energy in the aura, not that an 'unhealthy' aura is a symptom of physical illness. Consequently she concentrates her treatment on the aura, not on the affected part, if that is the way the ailment presents itself.

MAGIC BULLETS

Rose Gladden is one of but a handful of healers who do not depend on a spiritualist interpretation of their gift. However, the evidence suggests that whether or not the healer considers the effect to be mediated

Right: *The intercession of a saint effects a cure for one of the faithful, as depicted in a 16th-century print. A secular interpretation would suggest that the cure comes about through the power of mind and emotions over the body rather than through divine intervention, but the effects, which are often dramatic, are the same.*

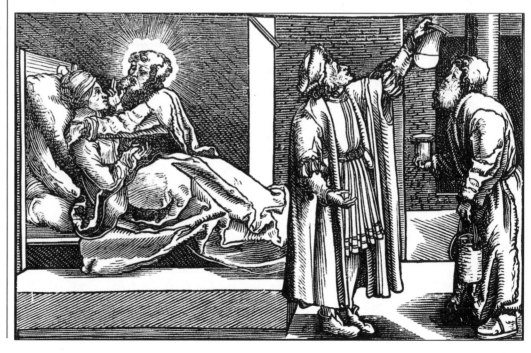

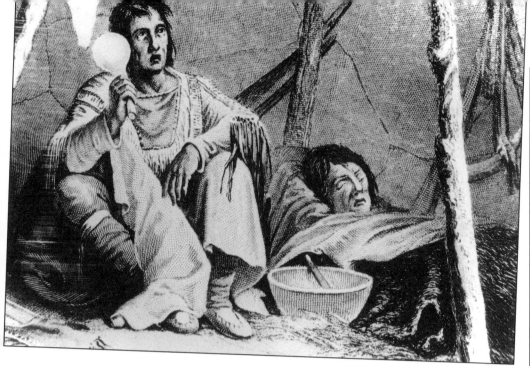

Left: *An Ojibway American Indian medicine man, or shaman, at work. Shamanistic healing centres on the patient's spirit – or on evil spirits within the sufferer's body – in order to cure physical ills. Sickness is seen as a symptom of the state of the soul, not merely a bodily condition demanding a purely physical cure.*

Below: *Conventional medicine is beginning to recognize that a patient kept confident and in good spirits will heal more quickly than one treated like an item on a production line.*

by the spirit world, or is directly from God (as with faith healers), or that he or she simply acts as a channel for a 'universal life force', the effects are the same: a very high proportion of the people who take their ailments to healers are cured.

Whatever the explanation or the source for the *healer's* powers, this would suggest that the state of the patient's mind, at least, has a massive degree of control over the state of the body. Part of the healing process, in other words, seems to depend on the confidence and reassurance that people gain by putting themselves entirely in the healer's hands. In effect, they heal themselves, as responsibility for the affliction is taken out of their hands and placed in someone else's.

Yet something more than this seems to be happening with psychic healing, and anyone might reasonably object to such a line of argument, not least an orthodox general practitioner. By taking an illness to a doctor you are also putting yourself in someone else's hands, even though conventional medicine addresses physical problems with physical methods such as surgery, or with physical tools, such as drugs, which are aimed like 'magic bullets' at the physical causes of specific ailments.

There is no doubt that in most cases, given an accurate diagnosis, conventional medicine works. The patient has entrusted a specifically physical malady to the doctor, and the doctor finds the physical cure. To that extent, mind and body are as one. But the exclusively physical approach does not always work. Given the mira- culous subtlety and complexity of the human body, and also the largely unfathomed intricacy of its relationship with the mind and with the emotions, this failure is not entirely surprising. Furthermore, conventional medicine traditionally regards *symptoms* as the clue to the underlying causes, and tackles those first.

If healers succeed where conventional

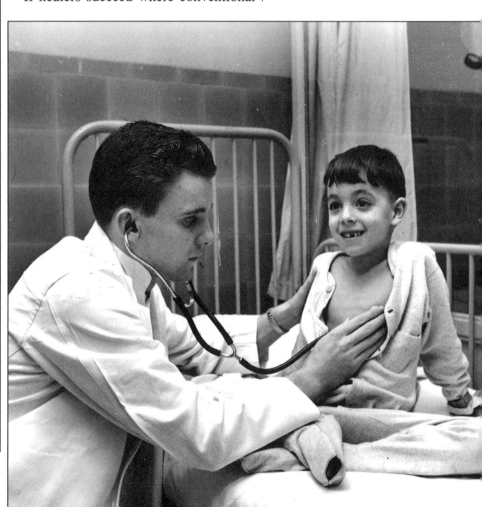

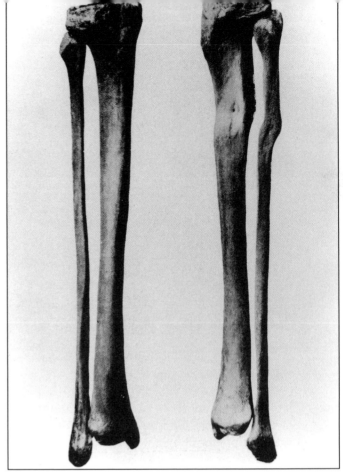

Belgian Pierre de Rudder (above, photographed in 1893) had one leg broken when a tree fell on him in 1867. He refused to have the damaged leg amputated and was in constant agony until April 1875, when he made a pilgrimage to the shrine of Our Lady of Lourdes at Oostaker, Belgium, where the pain miraculously vanished. Despite the distortion in his bones (above right, in a post-mortem photograph), De Rudder thereafter walked normally and with perfect ease until his death in 1898.

medicine fails, it may be partly because the patients entrust something different – something not merely physical, and something more than the physical symptoms of disease – to the healer. By accepting the reality and the importance of the interplay among mind, spirit and the emotions, and the part they may be playing in the illness, the patients implicitly put their whole being in the hands of the healer. And the healer, unlike the family GP or the specialist consultant, knows how to respond.

SERIOUSLY DISTURBED

This line of argument still supposes that suggestion plays a large part in the healer's art. However, as noted a few sentences earlier, something more seems to be happening when psychic healing takes place. When Rose Gladden laid her hands on the place where a bright light told her Mr Chapman's ulcer was, there was no 'suggestion' involved: neither Chapman nor Rose Gladden herself knew that she had the power to heal. And one of the wonders of psychic healing is that it can often deal with diseases that are intractable to modern medicine, such as cancer or multiple sclerosis.

Walter J. Kilner observed that the human aura reflected a person's state of health, and noted that 'weak depleted auras suck off the auric energy of healthy, vigorous auras around them'. Unhealthy parts of the aura, or the spirit, or one's general sense of well-being, will feed on the more vigorous parts in exactly the same way; but the overall effect is to disturb the system. The same is true of all energy systems: power moves from areas of high energy into areas of low energy, in an eternal and perfectly natural struggle to create and maintain a balance in nature.

You can see the same thing happening across the Earth's surface, nightly on the television weather forecast. Areas of low atmospheric pressure are fed by areas of high pressure in an attempt to even things out; the result in temperate climates is wind, cold fronts, rain…and the occasional spell of fine and balmy weather. An aura – or a person's psyche, or energy lines and meridians, or what you will – will constantly fluctuate in this way, but can, like the weather, become seriously disturbed. In meteorological terms, such a major disturbance in the balance of energies expresses itself as a storm or a drought; in terms of personal health, it means illness. And what, by all accounts,

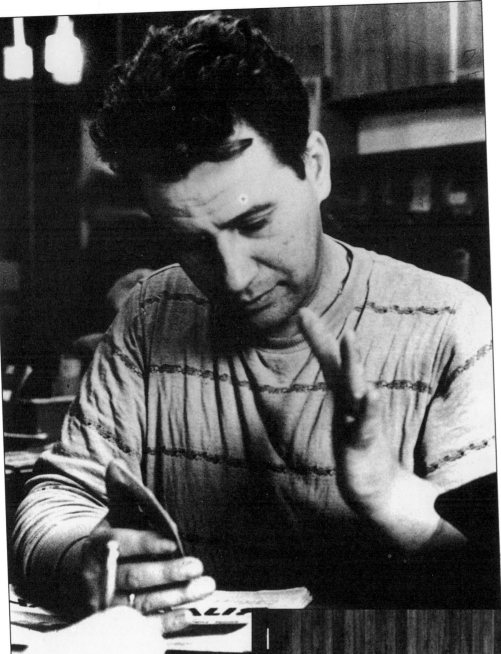

Psychic healing may be practised at a distance, or directly. Russian healer Alexandr Ilyin of St Petersburg makes diagnoses from photographs of his patients (left), while John F. Thie's technique, known as 'Touch for Health' (below), uses direct manipulation as part of the therapy.

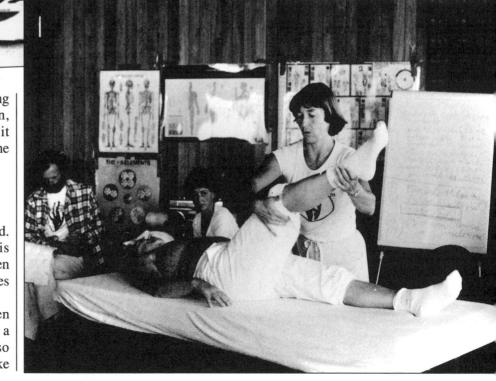

the healer does, is the equivalent of giving a troubled body an energy transfusion, which rights the balance – which, as it were, calms the storm or brings rain to the parched earth.

HIDDEN POWERS

The mystery in psychic healing is twofold. Exactly what that energy consists of is anyone's guess. And how it can work even when the healer may be thousands of miles from the sufferer is equally inexplicable.

The sensation that patients most often report feeling when they are touched by a healer is that of heat. Patients have also described tingling feelings, 'something like

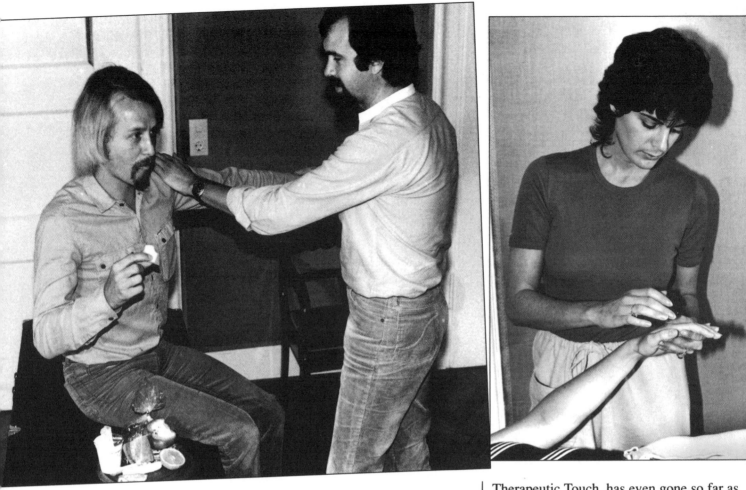

'Touch for Health' diagnoses involve testing for reactions to certain foods (above) *and kinesiological testing* (above right).

CAYCE REALIZED THAT THE STRANGE GIFT WAS OUT OF HIS CONTROL.

an electric shock', or even vivid impressions of colours before the eyes as the healer has touched them. At the same time, according to the Harper's *Encyclopedia* quoted earlier, healers have reported 'something of the consistency of heavy air' – whatever that may mean in practice – departing them, usually through the hands. The spiritualist healer Ambrose Worrall, in contrast, felt himself depleted of energy, indeed, but through the solar plexus.

These reports are both too various and too subjective to allow much of a guess as to what in fact has passed between the parties involved. And, intriguing and possibly helpful as they are, descriptions of what occurs in terms of the human aura really amount to explaining one mystery in terms of another. Only a relatively few people can see the aura, and they differ in their descriptions and analyses of it; it has stubbornly remained undetected by orthodox scientific means.

That something does pass between healer and healed seems to be beyond doubt, however. Dora van Gelder Kunz, a pioneer of a modern form of healing called Therapeutic Touch, has even gone so far as to suggest that there is actually a two-way interaction between healer and patient, and that in the process both are made more whole and healthy.

THE FINAL HEALING

The mystery of psychic healing is only deepened by the ability of certain healers to treat their patients at a distance – even without meeting them.

The most famous exponent of distant healing was probably Edgar Cayce. Born in Hopkinsville, Kentucky, in 1877, Cayce followed the pattern of many other healers in being able to discern non-physical forms, and the human aura, from an early age. Until he was 21 he worked as a salesman, but had to abandon his job because of a chronic and apparently incurable sore throat, made worse by bouts of laryngitis. In 1898, Cayce lost his voice completely and, as a last resort, went to hypnotist Al Layne in the hope of getting some relief from his distressing condition.

Layne concluded that Cayce was immune to post-hypnotic suggestion (a command given during hypnosis to be carried out in the normal waking state), so he put Cayce into trance and asked him to identify the cause of his illness, and to suggest a cure himself. The ploy worked: Cayce was able to speak again at the end of the session. Layne suggested that Cayce should take up diagnosis and healing himself, in partnership with Layne.

Cayce refused, and promptly lost his voice again. Taking this as a sign that healing others was to be his destiny, he began to give readings – diagnoses and cures while in trance – in 1901. A key factor in Cayce's gift was that whenever he used it against his own principles – and he was a devout Christian – or even gave up readings, he would lose his voice. In this respect, and like many other psychics, Cayce was not entirely in control of his strange talent. He did not direct it; rather, it seemed to use him as a channel.

Thanks to a newspaper article about him in 1903, Cayce found a large following, and this increased still further in 1911 when a feature on his work – and his successes – in the *New York Times* brought him to national attention. By this time he was working in partnership with Dr Wesley Ketchum, a homoeopath who carried out the treatment that Cayce prescribed.

Cayce had begun his work by being hypnotized in the presence of the patient; now he needed no more than the name and address of the patient, and to put himself into trance. The reading would begin when someone (often Cayce's wife) would tell him: 'You now have the body of [here the name and address was read out]. You will go over this body carefully, noting its condition and any parts that are ailing. You will give the cause of such ailments and suggest treatments to bring about a cure.'

Cayce believed that every single cell in the body was individually conscious, and maintained not only that during a reading he could see every nerve, gland, blood vessel and organ inside his patient's body, but that the cells themselves communicated their condition to his entranced mind. The treatments he prescribed ranged from orthodox drugs or surgery (Cayce had no objection to conventional medicine where it was appropriate) through massage, manipulation, osteopathy and electro-therapy to herbal remedies (some of

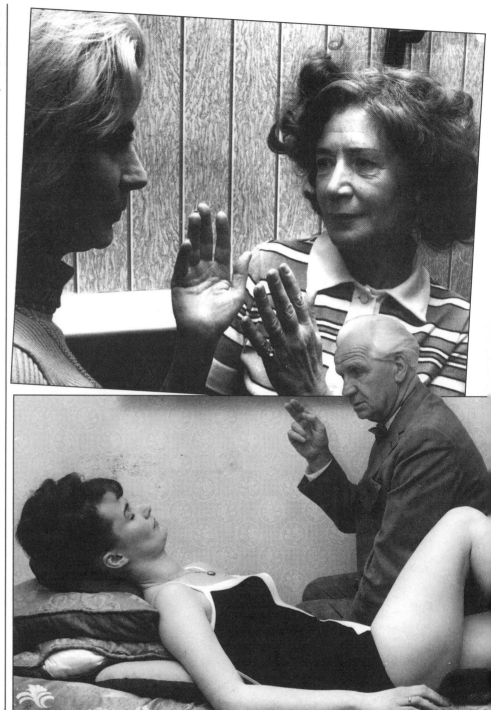

remarkable obscurity) and plain, simple exercise. The effectiveness of his pre-scriptions was vouched for by thousands of patients.

Many of Cayce's later ideas have been mocked – perhaps with some justice – for their outlandishness. For example, he came to believe that he himself was a reincarnation of one of the angels who inhabited the Earth even before Adam and Eve, and later was incarnated as an inhabitant of Atlantis. But as a healer he

One of the most widely used methods of putting the mind in control of the body is hypnotism. Doris Munday (top) specializes in treating nervous tension, while Harry Blythe (above) is seen here curing a would-be beauty queen of shyness.

Edgar Cayce's more extreme ideas – that he had been a citizen of the mythical lost continent of Atlantis (right) in a previous incarnation, and that still earlier he had been an angel existing 'before Adam and Eve' (below) – have been mocked as outlandish, but they did not affect his ability to give healing at a distance.

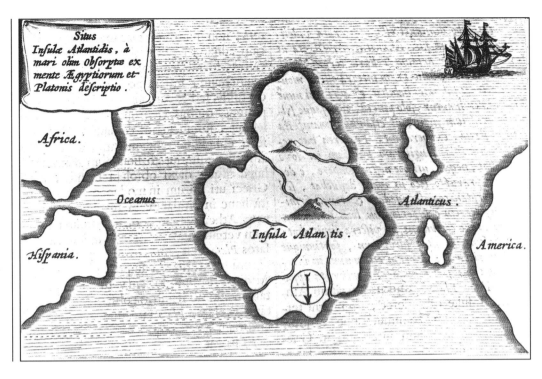

HE KNEW THAT TOO MANY HEALINGS WOULD KILL HIM, BUT HOW COULD HE IGNORE THE SUFFERINGS CAUSED BY THE WAR?

has had few equals.

The transfer of energy typical of healing took its toll on Cayce, who found the work exhausting. Warned that giving more than two readings a day would kill him, he nevertheless averaged four each day after 1942, in response to requests that flooded in as a result of the USA joining the war against Germany and Japan. In June 1943, he increased this to six a day; in August 1944 he collapsed from exhaustion, and was dead within five months. He had referred to his impending death as a 'healing'.

UNCANNY PRECISION

The most celebrated British clairvoyant healer was probably Harry Edwards, who died in 1976. During his prime in the 1950s he could fill London's giant Albert Hall with people anxious to receive his services. Edwards did not invoke spirit guides or use any ritual, whether healing at such a huge gathering or at home. He simply rolled up his sleeves and for a few moments put his hands on whatever part of the body was troubling the patient.

Astonishingly, Edwards took up healing virtually by chance. He seems to have had no inkling of any psychic capacities as a young man, and he was already in his forties when he made his first attempt at healing – and that was at a distance. This he did only after he had attended Spiritualist church services to please a friend. At these, he was told by a number of mediums that he had a latent ability as a healer, and that next time he knew someone who was ill, he should concentrate his thoughts on his or her recovery.

Edwards heard that a friend of a friend was terminally ill with tuberculosis, and decided to do what he could to help the man. He simply sat down and began to meditate. Then, images came into his mind of a hospital ward, and he found himself concentrating on the occupant of the last

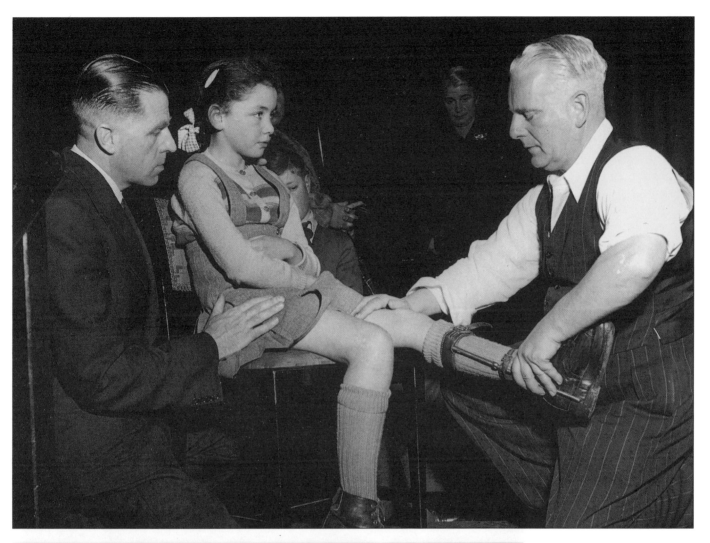

In the 1950s Harry Edwards (above) was Britain's foremost healer, and his fame was so widespread that he was able to fill the 8000-seat Royal Albert Hall (left) to capacity for his demonstrations.

Right: *Greek gendarme Costas Polychronakis is hypnotized and cured of a spinal disease by Harry Edwards during a brief stop that the healer made at Athens airport in April 1954.*

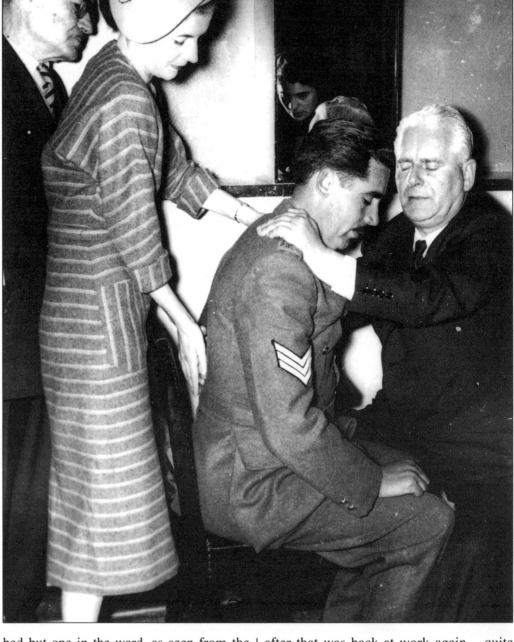

SHE WAS SCARED HE WOULD MOCK HER INTUITION AND NEVER CONFESSED HER SECRET.

bed but one in the ward, as seen from the point of view in his mind. Edwards sent out a 'get well' message as powerfully as he could, although without great confidence in its likely efficacy.

However, when Edwards described the scene he had had in his mind to his friend, he found that he had 'imagined' the ward in the hospital and the circumstances of the TB victim with uncanny precision. Better still, the patient had reported feeling better almost immediately after Edwards had made his attempt at healing. Within a few weeks the man was up and about, and soon

after that was back at work again – quite confounding his doctors, who had fully expected him to die.

The next encounter Edwards had with his paranormal gift – and it was one that lends some credence to the suspicion that the lives, let alone the talents, of healers are somehow beyond their control – came not long after this. Harry Edwards lived in Islington, London, and worked in a printing shop in the neighbourhood. One day a woman came into the shop, obviously distracted and, admitting she had no reason for bursting in, poured out her story to

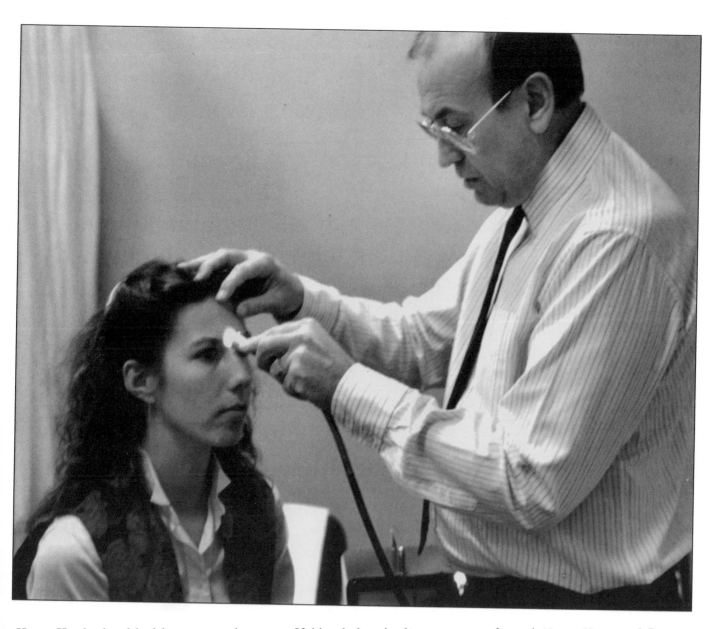

Harry. Her husband had lung cancer in an advanced degree: he was so far gone that he had been sent home from hospital – in short, to die.

Edwards personally believed there was little he could do to help (there was *nothing* he could do about the unfathomable way in which the distressed woman had found him), but made an effort nonetheless. Two days after her first visit, the woman dropped into the printing shop again. Her husband, she said, had already begun to recover. And recover he did: he lived for a score more years. The curious irony of this case was that he himself never learned of the part that Harry Edwards may have had in his sudden return to normal life. His wife never told him of her strange impulse to walk into a printing shop in Islington, for fear he would mock her intuition.

If this whole episode was no more than a crazy coincidence, it was fortunate as well as fortuitous. Edwards's third attempt at healing was also unusual, for it was the first time he actually had physical contact with his patient, a young girl suffering from TB of the lung. What marked the occasion for Edwards was what happened when he put his hands on the girl's head. He had experienced nothing of the kind before: his entire body seemed to come alive, filled with energy, which flooded down his arms and out of his hands into the patient. When this extraordinary sensation ceased, he heard himself telling the girl's mother that her daughter would be up in three days. Indeed she was, and at her next medical examination was pronounced completely cured.

These three events convinced Edwards

Above: *Naturopath Peter Mandel of Bruchsal, Germany, uses coloured light beams instead of needles to apply his own form of acupuncture to his patients.*

Right: *Diagnosis by dowsing, as employed by healer Nicola Cutolo of Italy. Cutolo also uses dowsing for more orthodox purposes – among them finding the location of missing persons.*

that he should devote himself to healing; in due course, he gave up his printing business and in 1946 established a sanctuary at Burrows Lea in Shere, Surrey, to carry on his work full-time. He was still working when he died in 1976. The sanctuary still thrives, run by a group of healers.

INEXPLICABLE PROOF

A number of healers have collaborated in tests to discover if there is any 'objective' element in what they do. The British healer Matthew Manning, for instance, has been involved in this research, attempting to influence the growth rate of seedling plants, to destroy cancer cells in the laboratory, and to increase the enzyme level in samples of blood. Testing on items like these removes the possibility that they may respond as a result of their own suggestibility – which may account for a

healer's success with human patients.

Much work along these lines was done by the biochemist Bernard Grad of McGill University in Montreal, Canada, during the 1950s. His research with the retired Hungarian army colonel Oskar Estebany was particularly revealing. Estebany had discovered his own healing ability by working not with people, but with horses of the Hungarian cavalry.

Grad tested the healer's ability to influence the growth of barley seeds successfully, but he performed one crucial experiment with Estebany. One involved 'wounding' a number of laboratory mice (actually just a tiny sliver of skin was painlessly removed from each one). Sixteen of the 48 animals were given healing treatment by being held in Estebany's hands twice a day for 20 days. Another 16 were put in incubators heated to body temperature for the same period twice a day, to simulate the warmth the first

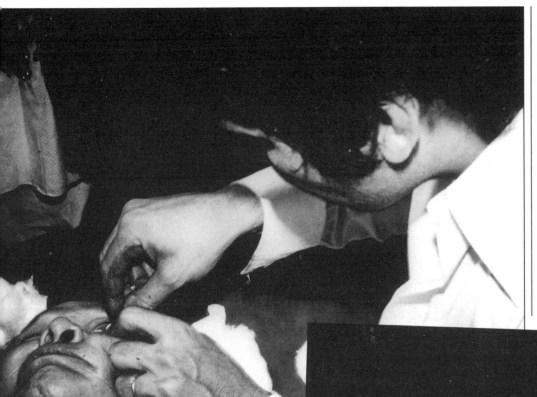

Left and below: *Ivan Trilha of Paraguay performs psychic surgery. Using neither anaesthetics nor conventional surgical instruments, psychic surgeons claim to be able to perform all the feats of modern medicine. Many of their patients have testified to the effectiveness of their work – but just as many of the 'surgeons' have been exposed as charlatans.*

group received from Estebany. A third group of 16 mice provided a final control: they were left to heal naturally.

By day 14 of the experiment, the size of the wounds of the control group had diminished as expected: about a third had reduced to less than half their original size, and the remainder were smaller yet. Of the 'heated' group, about half had reduced to about half their initial size; if anything, the group as a whole was healing more slowly than the control group – not surprisingly, since warmth encourages the multiplication of bacteria. Estebany's group had healed faster than either of the others: their three biggest wounds were smaller than *one-seventh* the size they had been initially; the rest were equal in size or (more often) smaller than those of the untreated control group.

Grad and Estebany were no nearer explaining the mechanism of the healer's art than anyone else, but they had shown that it had a real effect on live animals – who could not be accused of 'healing themselves' through auto-suggestion, faith, or any other psychosomatic means.

OUT OF THE BODY

The torture was agony but Ed Morrell refused to be broken. Even as his cruel jailers slowly squeezed him to the jaws of death, he found a way to escape.

Ed Morrell had the bad luck to be incarcerated in the Arizona State Penitentiary, rated one of the four most savage jails in the USA. One of the more refined methods of torture that Morrell suffered there was to be tied into not one but two strait-jackets; then water was poured over him, so that the jackets shrank. It was, he wrote in his book *The Twenty Fifth Man*, like being 'slowly squeezed to death'. But, time and again, Morrell escaped from this agony: his consciousness – some would say his soul, others would call it his 'astral body' – left his body to suffer, and floated away, free from pain.

In this 'out-of-the-body' state, Morrell was able to travel not only around the immediate vicinity of the prison, but to other countries. He seems even to have been able to travel in time. On one disembodied journey he saw a woman that he later was to meet in the flesh – and marry.

Out-of-the-body experiences (OBEs) are often associated with escape from extreme physical pain, as in Morrell's case; victims of road accidents, for instance, have often reported that their conscious self has floated free from their broken bodies, so that they survey themselves from a point above (and often slightly to one side of) their physical position.

The British secret agent Odette Hallowes positively looked forward to her OBEs when she was captured and tortured by the Gestapo during World War 2. When the pain reached a certain intensity, she would literally rise above it, leaving the sadists 'below' her to get on with their inhuman work while she, now free from any physical feelings, felt a profound sense of relief.

DRUG-INDUCED?

It is not necessary, however, to suffer extreme stress, shock or trauma in order to have an OBE. The experience can happen spontaneously and without warning to someone who is especially relaxed. One such episode was reported by a florist known only as Pat who, when she was 20, in April 1970, shared a flat in Canterbury, Kent, with her musician cousin.

'I [was] lying on the sofa for a few hours, listening to my cousin play the piano. I was completely relaxed and felt as if I were going to sleep,' she recalled. 'Suddenly I was aware that I had actually risen to ceiling height. I turned over and seemed to hover…I could see everything in the room quite clearly, even myself lying on the sofa…I suddenly found myself way up in the sky hovering over Canterbury. Only it wasn't April any more; it was a summery day.

'I didn't want to return, indeed I had a great sense of elation. But…what would happen if I travelled on into the unknown? As I was thinking about this I found myself staring down at my body again. I decided I

Opposite: Wartime secret agent Odette Hallowes with two dolls that she made while a prisoner of the Nazi Gestapo. Under torture, she would escape the harrowing pain by floating free of her body.

Below: An attempt to induce an out-of-the-body experience using coloured eyeglasses and aural stimulation through headphones, conducted at the Freiburg Institute in Germany in 1982.

THE BRAVE SECRET AGENT DID NOT SUCCUMB TO HER SADISTIC TORTURERS.

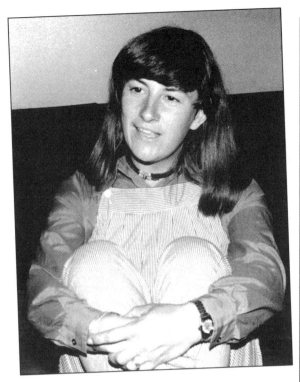

Psychologist Dr Susan Blackmore **(right)**, *who believes that OBEs are not actual journeys by the mind or spirit, but are created in the imagination.*

Keith Harary **(below)** *accurately reported details of distant locations – which he had never visited – during OBE experiments in the 1970s.*

essential to initiate this class of OBE. In 1971, psychologist Dr Charles Tart surveyed 150 regular smokers of marijuana and discovered that 44 per cent of them had had an OBE while using the drug. Other surveys have established that roughly one person in four has experienced an OBE at least once in their lives – suggesting that the state of fatuous euphoria typically associated with smoking dope increases the likelihood of you getting literally out of your head.

ASTRAL BODIES

These OBEs – brought on by intolerable physical stress or when the mind has, in effect, gone blank through relaxation or boredom – occur of their own accord; those who have them cannot control either their onset or, apparently, the way they end. But OBEs can be induced deliberately and enjoyed at will.

In their book *The Projection of the Astral Body* (1929), Sylvan Muldoon and Hereward Carrington describe several ways in which to achieve an OBE. All involve lying on your back in bed with the eyes closed. You might then concentrate on loosening the 'astral body' from the physical body, by rotating your point of view in the imagination around a central axis – so that you are looking at your own feet, for example, or at the length of your body. From these positions you should look at the ceiling, the wall on one side, the floor, and the wall on the other side.

Another suggestion is to hold the image and imaginary sensation of going up in a lift until you drift off to sleep, while telling yourself that you will wake up fully out of the body. A third method is to make sure you go to bed thirsty, and go to sleep while imagining going to the kitchen for a drink of water – and telling yourself to wake up, out of the body, at the sink. These methods do indeed work, although at first they take a great deal of concentration and willpower.

The fact that an OBE *can* be deliberately induced has meant that the true nature of the experience can be explored through tests and experiments. The first question to be answered, naturally enough, is: does the consciousness *really* leave the body during an OBE and wander about at will?

couldn't do it…as soon as I had made my decision I was back in my body before you could say "Jack Flash".'

Others have reported having an OBE as a result of sheer boredom – one lady office worker claimed she found her mind frequently drifting into a reverie during particularly tedious meetings, and she would find herself wondering, 'What's on the other side of that wall?' Then, she would 'float' out of her body, out of the meeting-room and 'have a good look round'. Relaxation and a relatively idle, non-concentrating conscious mind seem

The anecdotal evidence that this does actually happen is conflicting. In Pat's OBE, cited earlier, it is curious that once out of her own basement flat and apparently high in the sky above Canterbury, the weather changed from that of a normal April day in England (which means it was raining) to that of a sunny summer day. Dr Susan Blackmore, a world authority on OBEs, became intrigued by the subject because she had them herself. In one, she floated to the ceiling, through it and above the housetops of her neighbourhood. Looking down, she could see the red roofs and chimneys of the buildings below as she flew over them…In her down-to-earth analysis of the event, Dr Blackmore noted wryly that in fact the roofs she supposedly floated over were actually made of grey slate, and that none of the buildings in the district had chimneys like the ones she saw.

Dr Blackmore has also had an interesting response from an experiment set up with a friend who lives 200 miles from her and who claimed that he had OBEs regularly and could 'travel' long distances at will. To find out if he did travel in reality or in imagination, Dr Blackmore left three items on the top of a cupboard in her kitchen, out of sight of any casual visitor. They were a small object such as a comb or a piece of candy, a three-digit number, and a short word. The arrangement was that when her friend paid a flying visit during an OBE, he would check the top of the cupboard, note what was there, and send her a postcard describing what he had seen. Each week Dr Blackmore changed the three objects. She did this for five years. No postcard ever arrived.

TRAVELLING CLAIRVOYANCE

Others have reported entirely different experiences. The American medium Eileen Garrett, for example, tells in her autobiography how she carried out an experimental OBE at the request of a doctor who lived in Newfoundland. Garrett lived in New York, and had never been to the doctor's home. She projected herself from New York to the house in Newfoundland, and there saw the doctor, who was himself somewhat psychic and was apparently able to detect her arrival. She noted a number of objects laid out on the

doctor's table, and also saw that he had a bandaged head. He told her, speaking out loud, that he had had an accident that morning. Next, he pulled a book from a shelf and opened it so that she could read the title page.

All this information and more about what Garrett had seen during her out-of-the-body visit to Newfoundland was written down and mailed to the doctor the same day. Next day, he telegraphed a reply confirming everything Garrett had reported.

Here we have two diametrically different accounts of OBEs, both from people renowned for their honesty. How can we account for the apparent contradiction?

First, let's suppose that Dr Blackmore is correct in thinking an OBE is essentially an imaginary experience – a 'dramatized reconstruction of a memory of the physical world', in Prof. Arthur Ellison's words.

Second, Eileen Garrett was one of the most accomplished mediums of all time. It seems likely, then, that what she saw on her OBE to Newfoundland was correct not because she was spiritually or astrally there in person, but because she was there psychically. The modern term for what she was doing is 'remote viewing', a form of extra-sensory perception that used to be called 'travelling clairvoyance'. Telepathy may have been involved too, for the doctor in the experiment was also psychic.

Third, it is well-known among psychical researchers that Dr Blackmore herself is

Above: *A sentimental Victorian depiction of the astral body – synonymous with the spirit form of the dead – watching invisibly over the grief-stricken living.*

OUT-OF-THE-BODY EXPERIENCES CAN BE INDUCED DELIBERATELY, AND ENJOYED AT WILL.

Above: *Psychical researcher Helmut Schmidt demonstrates a random-event generator of his own devising, for use in experiments in psychokinesis. Some experts have suggested that out-of-the-body experiences enhance psychic ability.*

TWO INVISIBLE HANDS FORCED HIM BACK INTO THE BEDROOM AND DOWN INTO HIS BODY.

distinctly un-psychic; she has remarked ruefully on the fact that she actually seems to inhibit extra-sensory perception many times. Her own lack of psychic gifts and her tendency apparently to block others' extra-sensory perception would not only explain the discrepancies between her view of her neighbourhood during her OBE and the actual facts about the place. It would also account for her friend's being unable to discover what she had put on the top of her kitchen cupboard – either she was blocking him from getting at the information telepathically, or he himself has no talent for extra-sensory perception (or both).

We've seen from accounts of many other psychic phenomena that extra-sensory perception (like an OBE) is often triggered by a crisis. It's also apparent that both extra-sensory perception and OBEs can occur as a result of profound relaxation that amounts to a trance state. An OBE may not make someone without any latent psychic ability into a sensitive, but it may make a chink in his or her psychic armour; and to someone moderately sensitive who has many OBEs it may help their extra-sensory perceptions develop. Thus Ed Morrell could see his future wife during one of his repeated OBEs. He was having a precognitive vision.

Even if OBEs are not literally journeys of the soul out of the body, but an extraordinary facet of the imagination, they are nonetheless replete with unsolved mysteries.

INTRIGUING EXPERIENCE

There are many reports of the curious effects experienced during OBEs – by both those undergoing them, and those researching them. One such series of oddities was recounted by Dr Arthur Ellison, professor of electronic engineering at the City University, London, until 1986 and at one time a president of the British Society for Psychical Research.

Ellison had himself induced his own OBEs as an experiment, but abandoned this line of research simply because he was exhausted by the lack of sleep it entailed. He did have one very curious experience during his second OBE, however. He had succeeded in floating out of his bedroom window and was aiming to drift down to the lawn below, where he intended to walk about. (It is, incidentally, a peculiar quality of OBEs that those who have them seem to travel about with a sense of having a body of some kind: hence the term 'astral body' used in many discussions of the phenomenon.) Ellison was starting his descent to the ground when: 'I had one of the most intriguing experiences to date. I felt two hands take my head, one hand over each ear, [and] move me...back into the bedroom and down into the body. I heard no sound, and saw nothing.'

Ellison felt, on balance, that it was more likely that an OBE was an imaginative reconstruction of reality and not an actual paranormal mode of travel. But there remained the problem of people who picked up undoubtedly genuine information during OBEs that they had no other apparent means of having acquired. Ellison decided to test for the possibility that information of this kind was acquired telepathically.

For his experiments he had an electronic machine built. This would generate a random number and show it on a standard digital panel at the back. No one would see this number at any time during the experiment, except for the subject – and then only if they could read it during their OBE. On the front of the machine, a second display would record the number that the subjects claimed to see and show whether the claim was correct or not. It could also tell whether individual digits in the three-figure number had been read correctly. It still did not show the original number.

Ellison chose as his subjects people who could be hypnotized and would then have an OBE. The advantage of this system was that they could report from their physical state what their ostensibly disembodied selves were seeing. The machine could thus display runs of 20 or more numbers, giving the answers statistical validity.

MACHINE MALFUNCTION

There were two intriguing results of Ellison's experiments with this device. He first tested the machine with a female subject and, to speed up this initial informal trial, checked the psychic's claims by looking at the numbers at the back of the machine himself. She achieved a correct score of almost 100 per cent. But when a completely secure run of numbers was made, she scored zero, and made some rather feeble excuses about not being able to read the numbers properly because they were 'too small' – which, strange to say, had not been a problem before.

The obvious conclusion was that when no one was actually aware of the target figures, she could not see them. Or, to put it another way, she could identify the numbers only through someone else's awareness – that is, by telepathy.

On two further notable occasions Ellison tested well-known psychics with his machine. The first, an American, achieved a score of eight correct numbers out of 20 without even going into an OBE – about eight times any score that one might expect by chance guessing. When Ellison tested the machine the following day, he himself – who makes no claim to psychic ability at all – achieved the same astonishingly high score. Checking the guts of the device revealed a fault in the circuitry.

The British psychic came up with exactly the same high score. Then, in a control run, so did Ellison. Once again, apparently, the machine had malfunctioned. Ellison concluded: 'An experienced psychical researcher…might observe that this kind of thing often happens. It is as though the unconscious mind of the psychic, knowing that a high score was required, achieved this by the easiest available method – by using [psycho-kinesis] on the microcircuit rather than clairvoyance. But it is impossible to prove this contention: it merely remains a possibility.'

CRISIS APPARITIONS

No less mysterious are those rare cases in which subjects having an OBE actually appear in front of someone they are visiting in their disembodied state.

On 26 January 1957, just such an encounter took place between 26-year-old Martha Johnson and her mother. During an OBE, Martha 'floated' to her mother's house 926 miles away, in another time zone. When she arrived, she found her mother in the kitchen. Martha took a couple of steps toward her, but then came abruptly back to her body. She looked at her bedside clock: it read 2.10 am.

For her part, Martha's mother wrote to her at once to tell her own side of the story – and, when she did so, she had no idea that Martha had been having an OBE. She had noticed nothing at first, then gradually became aware of Martha standing in the kitchen in a typical posture: with her arms folded and her head slightly tilted to one side. She started to say something to her daughter – but then Martha abruptly vanished. She noted in her letter how good Martha's new hairstyle looked. The time she had seen her, she added, was 'ten after two, your time'.

There was no sense of crisis or foreboding in this experience; Martha's mother seems to have taken the whole episode in her stride. Only when both parties were about to put the situation to the test by communicating did it break down: as if psychic reality and the mundane world were incapable of co-existing.

THE SCORE WAS UNEXPECTEDLY HIGH – BUT JUST HOW HAD IT BEEN ACHIEVED?

Below: *Indian yoga adept Pushal Behen about to undergo an analysis of her brain-wave patterns with an electro-encephalograph. Out-of-the-body experiences are often deliberately induced by highly trained practitioners of yoga.*

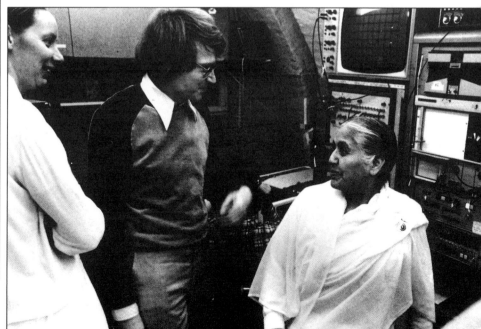

' Photograph of "vital radiations" issuing from the human body and impressing (directly) a photographic plate.

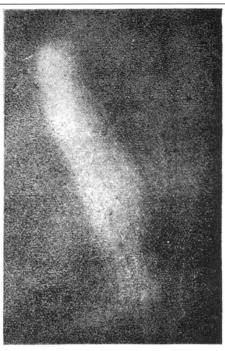

"Astral body" of Mme. Lambert obtained during the early experiments. (Note the imperfect outline of the body, and its swaying motion as though blown about by the wind.)

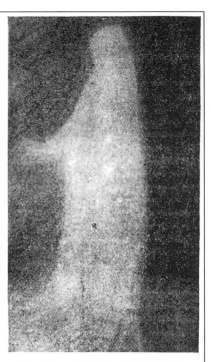

Later photograph of the "astral body." of Mme. Lambert, obtained after further experimentation. (Note the clearer outline and relative stability of the figure.)

Above: *These three photographs, published in the* **Occult Review** *of May 1916, purport to show the emergence of the astral body of one Madame Lambert from her physical form. Spiritualists and others remain convinced that it is the astral body which floats free of the body during an OBE.*

WHEN THEY RAN ROUND THE CORNER THE FIGURE OF THE SOLDIER HAD DISAPPEARED.

Circumstances were to say the least slightly different when Mr W. Lee of Bridgnorth, Shropshire, visited his mother in what seems to have been an OBE, in 1963. Lee was doing his stint of national service in the British Army at the time, and did not like it. He rebelled from time to time, and found himself at the mercy of an old Regular Army sergeant. He, on this occasion, landed Lee and three other conscripts with a punishment known by the innocuous name of 'pack drill'. At that time a standard infantryman's pack, fully loaded, weighed about 40 lb. Much of the kit inside was spare clothing. The sergeant ordered the four to fill their capacious packs not with issue kit but with housebricks, and then sent them out on the parade ground to drill with these back-breaking loads at a cracking pace.

It was a very hot day. One of the four kept collapsing. Lee, determined not to be beaten by the sadistic punishment, kept on marching. 'I just kept on going while the commands being shouted at us grew dimmer and dimmer,' he wrote years later. 'In the end I could not hear them. My heart did not seem to be beating and I could not see. Somehow I kept turning and marching but I was no longer there. Eventually the torture ended...'

That was all there was to that particular event, Lee thought, until the next time he returned home on leave. His mother then told him a curious tale.

On the same day that Lee had become an automaton on the drill square, his mother and his younger brother had been out shopping. 'They were about 100 yards from the nearest bus stop to our home,' he wrote, 'when a bus stopped and I got off in my Army uniform. [My mother] called to me as I walked up the road but I did not answer or turn round. It would be about 300 yards to the corner of our road, and my mother and brother...ran to try and catch me up, because I was walking very quickly. I rounded the corner four or five seconds ahead of them and when they too came round the corner I had disappeared. There was only a postman to be seen.

'My mother asked [him] where had the soldier gone and he told her nobody had come round the corner.'

In cases like these, the distinctions become blurred between what is an OBE, what is a *doppelganger* (the psychic double of a living person), and what is a 'crisis apparition' – the apparent ghost of someone who is, nonetheless, still alive. Even if most OBEs are the work of the imagination, incidents like these latter two show that we still only barely understand the phenomenon as a whole.